A NEW HISTORY OF MAURITIUS

John ADDISON

and

K. HAZAREESINGH

Revised Edition

EDITIONS DE L'OCEAN INDIEN

Published in 1984 by

Macmillan Publishers
London and Basingstoke
Companies and representatives in Lagos, Zaria, Manzini,
Nairobi, Singapore, Hong Kong, Delhi, Dublin, Auckland,
Melbourne, Tokyo, New York, Washington, Dallas

ISBN 0 333 34026 4
Reprinted in Mauritius in 1989 by the Editions de 1' Océan Indien
with the authorisation of Macmillan publishers.

Revised Edition : Kin Keong Printing (1993)
1st Reprint : Kin Keong Printing (1996)
2nd Reprint : Kin Keong Printing (1999)

Published by

Editions de l'Océan Indien
Stanley, Rose-Hill
Mauritius

ISBN 99903-0-166-2

To
Mr André Robert, CBE
Emeritous Sollicitor of Mauritius
for his outstanding contribution to the development and progress of Mauritius.

Aneerood Jugnauth Q.C., Prime Minister of Mauritius

CONTENTS

Acknowledgements

The author and publishers wish to acknowledge, with thanks, the following photographic sources.

Associated Press p 91
Barnaby's pp 13; 51
BBC Hulton Picture Library pp 2 right; 3 right; 34; 57
Bulloz 46
Camera Press pp 103; 109
J Allan Cash p 2 left
Central Press Photos pp 94; 95; 97
Jean-Loup Charmet pp 8; 9; 16; 43; 64
Compix pp 79; 102
Gerald Cubitt p 81
Mary Evans Picture Library p 20
F.A.O. Photo P. Morin p 107
Foreign and Commonwealth Office pp 70; 74
K. Hazareesingh pp 32; 45; 66; 75; 84; 85; 100; 105; 113
Keystone pp 80; 87
Mansell Collection pp 28; 42
National Maritime Museum p 41
Royal Geographical Society p 3 left
Roger Viollet pp 22; 73

The publishers have made every effort to trace the copyright holders, but if they have inadvertently overlooked any, they will be pleased to make the necessary arrangements at the first opportunity.

The authors and publishers also wish to thank the following who have kindly given permission for the use of copyright material:

Ministry of Economic Planning and Development, Mauritius for extracts from **"Mauritius Economic Review, 1971-1975"** 1976

Oxford University Press for extracts from **"A Descriptive Account of Mauritius, Its Scenery, Statistics, etc."** quoted in **"A New System of Slavery"** by Hugh Tinker, published for the Institute of Race Relations, 1974.

Cover : *Old print showing the 1st Dutchmen settling on the island whilst a couple of soldiers take a ride on the giant tortoises which were destroyed in the same way as the birds that are seen being slaughtered.*

PREFACE

Although this book has been written primarily with secondary school pupils in mind, and especially those who are preparing for the History of Mauritius Paper of the Cambridge School Certificate, it should also be of interest to other students and to the general reader. Most existing histories tell only part of the story or tell it unevenly and patchily. This is one of the first attempts to write a balanced, general history of the country.

The sections at the end of each chapter are meant for those who will use the book in schools. The *Suggestions for revision* guide pupils to the most important themes in each chapter. Those who follow up the *Suggestions for further work* will usually need some help and guidance from their teachers. It is hoped that these suggestions may point teachers to ideas for individual work by pupils which will lead to a fuller understanding of the story and, at times, to some appreciation of how to assess evidence and how to go about discovering evidence for themselves.

In my contribution to the writing of the book I have been much indebted to others who have worked on parts of the story before. In particular I have taken material and ideas from the works of Professor Hugh Tinker who has written three major works and numerous articles on the subject of Indian emigrants. I hasten to add that any deficiencies, whether errors of fact or controversial statements, are my responsibility alone.

J.F.A.
London

INTRODUCTION

In writing a history of Mauritius and of its people, we have tried to keep the balance equal between the various elements and forces that make up the nation. It has been brought up to date by covering the first twelve years of independence.

It is always difficult to maintain a sufficiently detached attitude in writing contemporary history. But it is so important that young people should form an objective view of the events in their country's recent past. However difficult the task, the attempt has to be made.

In my *History of Indians in Mauritius* I have covered some of these momentous changes. In this more comprehensive work the aim has been to get that part of the story in its proper perspective. With a view to achieving this objective I have received the invaluable help and collaboration of John Addison who has long experience in teaching and teacher training and who has been able to provide the necessary professional touch in the unfolding of the story of our island home. His contribution has been no less valuable in that the book has profited from his independent outlook and judgement; more than would have been possible for a Mauritian author who has been so closely involved in many events of the last forty-five years which have been decisive in shaping our country's destiny.

This book has the further advantage of conforming to the syllabus prescribed by the Cambridge Syndicate and the authors hope that both teachers and students will find it useful.

In the preparation of this book I have received the co-operation of many people who in one way or other have been associated with problems of historical development in Mauritius. While it would be difficult to mention all of them by name, I should like to record my gratitude to Sir Dayanand Burrenchobay, Sir Raman Osman, Sir Emile Séries and to Dr Régis Chaperon who, as Minister of Education, took the first step of introducing the teaching of Mauritian History in our Secondary Schools. I have also had the benefit of discussing some of the important topics with heads of schools and teachers and in particular with Mr Surendra Bissoondoyal who kindly placed his wide educational experience at my disposal.

Finally I should also like to thank Mrs S. Derpalsing, Miss Huguette Ly Tio Fane, Mrs Sooryakanty Gayan, Mrs Vimla Seebarrun and Mr Yves Chan Kam Lon for their help and assistance.

K Hazareesingh
St Antony's College, Oxford

NOTE TO THE SECOND EDITION

Historical research moves forward with the passage of time. The Second Edition takes account of more recent work on the Indian and Chinese diaspora. A whole new section has been added to chapter 10 – "Indian immigration and the growth of the Indian community in Mauritius", dealing more specifically with the causes of migration from India. And there is a whole new chapter that tells the story of Chinese immigration to Mauritius. Finally, with a view to increasing interest amongst secondary school pupils, I have attempted to update the book in the light of political, economic and social developments in Mauritian society since 1983. Although these changes represent my own personal contribution to this work, I would once again like to thank John Addison with whom I have greatly enjoyed writing this history. And a special word of thanks, once again to Mr Surendra Bissoondoyal, Chairman of Les Editions de l'Océan Indien and to Sadhna Ramlallah for their help in publishing this new edition.

Kissoonsingh Hazareesingh
Green College,
University of Oxford,
September 1993.

CHAPTER 1

Introduction: geographical background and early exploration

Mauritius is a predominantly green island with a considerable area of rocky volcanic mountains. These run roughly from north-east to south-west and rise to a height of well over 2000 feet in the south. Some of the sharply rising peaks look much higher than this and the land in their vicinity is so steep and rocky that neither crops nor any other vegetation will grow there. The lower slopes of the mountains are covered with forests and grassland. Most of the rest of the island, nearly 40 per cent of its area, is today covered with sugar cane fields which give it its dominant soft green colour. The soil is fertile and water supplies are good; but over the years vast quantities of rocks and boulders have been moved to make way for sugar cultivation. Mauritius possesses almost nothing of value in the way of natural resources or raw materials. It lies in the path of destructive cyclones which periodically cause widespread devastation to crops and property.

Those who have visited the island over the years have often depicted it in glowing and idyllic terms. In 1629 Thomas Herbert, an English writer and one of the first Englishmen to visit Mauritius, described it as 'an island paradise', a phrase used today in many tourist advertisements. In the nineteenth century the American author Mark Twain once said that God made Mauritius first and then modelled Heaven on the island. The fact that it took so long for men and women to settle there in any significant numbers, however, suggests that it was more difficult to live there permanently than to pay a short visit as an early 'tourist' or member of a visiting ship's crew.

Today Mauritius is one of the world's most densely populated countries and its population is one of the world's most culturally mixed. Yet the island had no indigenous people and it is less than 400 years since the first of its inhabitants settled there. It is very isolated: 500 miles from Madagascar, over 1000 miles from the nearest point on the East African coast and 2000 miles from India. It is this isolation which partly explains why it remained uninhabited for so long.

The first people to attempt to settle in Mauritius were the Dutch in the seventeenth century. The history of Mauritius effectively begins with these Dutch settlers of the seventeenth century. Long before that date, nearly a thousand years before the birth of Christ, it is possible that Phoenician sailors, setting out from what is today the Gulf of Aqaba, may have sailed into the southern parts of the Indian Ocean and visited Mauritius. If they did, however, we have no records to confirm it. In the fourth and fifth centuries A.D. Polynesians may have visited the island in their canoes on their way to settle in Madagascar. Again, however, there is no proof that they did so.

Arab traders

It is necessary to move on to the end of the first millenium A.D. before we have reliable evidence that traders were active in the vicinity of Mauritius. Arab merchants certainly began trading with the East African coast as far south as Mozambique and the Comoro Islands well before 1000 A.D. By mingling with African peoples on that coast they built up a new culture and civilisation known as the Swahili culture. This was the product of the mixing of Arab and African people, their languages and their ways of life.

Arab and Swahili traders visited the Comoro Islands and Madagascar and from the evidence of early maps they also seem to have visited the Seychelles and the Mascarenes. These two groups of islands are marked on medieval Arab maps. Rodrigues is called Dina arabi, Mauritius is Dina mozare and Réunion is Dina margabim. None of these people attempted to settle on any of these islands. They were first

An Arab dhow

and foremost traders and since the islands were all uninhabited, there were no possibilities for trading. Moreover it was dangerous for the Arab and Swahili sailors to venture regularly as far into the Indian Ocean as the Mascarene islands in their small ships, the triangular-sailed 'dhows' or 'sambouks'.

Eventually the Arabs controlled a rich trading empire stretching in a great arc around the shores of the Indian Ocean, from the East African coast to Indonesia via Arabia, Persia, India and Malaysia. In carrying on their trade with this empire they kept as close as possible to the main coastline, though they were aware of, and used, the steady seasonal monsoon winds for voyages across the Indian Ocean.

It was the desire of Christian Europe, for a combination of reasons, to attack and eventually take over this Muslim trading empire that led the European powers for the first time into the Indian Ocean. For the first Europeans, the Portuguese, it was, partly at least, a religious crusading spirit which lay behind their voyages of exploration and conquest in the fifteenth and sixteenth centuries. The most powerful motive, however, which drove others to follow, was the prospect of profit from the valuable trade of the area.

Portuguese exploration and trade

In 1498 the Portuguese explorer Vasco da Gama rounded the Cape of Good Hope and entered the Indian Ocean. He called at some of the Arab-Swahili cities as he sailed northwards up the East African coast and from Malindi an Arab pilot showed him the way to Goa in India. In the next few years other Portuguese expeditions followed. The East African cities from Sofala, in modern Mozambique, to Mogadishu, near the Horn of Africa in modern Somalia, were taken over, if necessary by force. In 1510 the Portuguese captured Goa and in 1511 Malacca in Malaysia. The way to the Spice Islands and China lay open to them.

In East Africa they eventually abandoned the northern section of the coast and Mozambique became their main base. Their route to India was via the Mozambique Channel. It was known as the 'inner route'. Though their ships, whether the light 'caravels' or the heavier 'carracks', were more suited to voyages in the

A Portuguese caravel of the fifteenth century

open oceans than the Arab 'dhows', the Portuguese followed the traditional monsoon routes to and from India which had been used by Arab sailors for centuries. The Portuguese were skilled navigators, many of them trained in the famous school of navigation founded by Prince Henry the Navigator at Sagres in the south-west of Portugal. Their captains charted the Indian Ocean. They 'discovered' Madagascar, the Comoros and the Seychelles within ten years of rounding the Cape. For a short time they attempted to establish a base on the Comoros but the islanders, who were staunch Muslims, were hostile and the Portuguese withdrew. Fernandez Pereira sighted Mauritius in 1507 and gave it the name of his ship, Cerne. The island and its near neighbours were given the name of the Mascarenes after another Portuguese captain, Pero Mascarenhas. The number of islands with Portuguese names in the area is an indication of the importance of the Portuguese contribution to the exploration of the Indian Ocean.

Dutch traders

In spite of this, the Portuguese showed no interest in colonising any of the small groups of islands. They soon had more than enough to do in merely holding on to the scattered bases which protected their new trade routes. Before 1600 the Dutch and the English had followed the Portuguese into the Indian Ocean. They both established East India Companies, the English in 1600 and the Dutch in 1602, to monopolise the trade of the two countries with India and the vast area between the Cape of Good Hope and Cape Horn. In 1598 a Dutch admiral, van Warwyck, called at Mauritius with a small expedition and took possession of the island in the name of the Dutch. They called it Mauritius in honour of Prince Maurice of Nassau, a member of the House of Orange and Stadtholder of Holland. At the time the Dutch were in rebellion against the Spanish and Portugal was ruled by the King of Spain. Portuguese ships and trade and Portuguese possessions were, therefore, targets for the Dutch ships in the Indian Ocean. Though they had claimed Mauritius as a Dutch possession, the Dutch made no attempt to settle or colonise the island for some years. In the meantime English, Dutch and, soon, French ships occa-

Don Pero Mascarenhas

Maurice of Nassau, Prince of Orange 1567-1625

sionally used the island as a port of call for their vessels. They were all interested in trade rather than territory at that time.

During the first half of the seventeenth century the Dutch built up an unchallenged supremacy in Indonesia and the Spice Islands. Their rivals, the English and the Portuguese, were forced to recognise this Dutch supremacy, and the islands now making the state of Indonesia became known as the Dutch East Indies. The main Dutch base was established in Batavia in Java in 1619. The English and the Portuguese, driven out of this area, continued to trade alongside the Dutch in India. The route to India followed by the Dutch and the English passed close to the Mascarene islands. This route was developed after 1611 and became known as the 'great route'. As a result the number of ships calling at Mauritius increased and they soon included French as well as Dutch and English ships. They took on supplies of food and fresh water. Occasionally they repaired their vessels. The island had plentiful supplies of timber, including ebony. Trees were often felled and the valuable cargo was taken off. European commercial activity in the Indian Ocean was rapidly building up and the rivalry and competition between the four main powers was increasing. Although they were all primarily interested in trade, this was a period when it was normal for each power to try to establish a monopoly of trade with a certain area. It was obvious that each power needed to establish and maintain bases if its merchants' trading rights were to be protected.

Suggestions for further work

1 Find out more about Portuguese and Arab ships of the period. In what ways were the Portuguese and other European ships superior to those of the Arab sailors of the period?

2 Who was Maurice of Nassau and for what reasons did he became famous as a leader of the Dutch?

3 Mark on a map of the Indian Ocean the main trading places occupied by the Portuguese in the early sixteenth century.
Make a list of the main items of trade carried by merchants in the Indian Ocean at this time.

4 Make sure you understand the meaning of the following words: indigenous and millenium (page 1), crusading (page 2), monopoly and Stadtholder (page 3).

CHAPTER 2

The Dutch in Mauritius, 1638-1710

Reasons for settling

In order to protect its trading rights by establishing a strategic base, the Dutch East India Company decided to send an expedition in 1638 to make a settlement on Mauritius. They feared that if they did not take this step the English or the French would do so. The French had so far no base in the Indian Ocean except at Fort Dauphin on Madagascar. They were known to be looking for a more suitable base. The English had acquired the right to a trading station at Surat in India and were soon to obtain similar rights near Madras in 1639.

The first Dutch governor of Mauritius, Cornelius Gooyer, had only twenty-five men under his control and was given a formidable list of assignments to try to carry out. He was to prevent the English and the French from making any further use of the island. He was to ensure that food was available for Dutch ships calling at Mauritius, and for this purpose was to grow crops and keep cattle and poultry. Tobacco also was to be grown and ebony and ambergris were to be reserved for export to Holland. In addition it was intended that the island should be used as a convalescent base for Dutch settlers and officials who became sick in Batavia. One of the advantages of the new settlement was that, in contrast to Java and the other islands in the Dutch East Indies, it had a healthy climate and was free from diseases.

The first Dutch settlement

The Dutch settlement was made at the spot where Admiral van Warwyck had landed forty years earlier near Grand Port Bay in the south-east corner of the island. A fort was built and named Warwyck Haven and a second smaller garrison was based in the north-west of the island near modern Port Louis to prevent foreign ships from using the natural anchorage there. This place was known, under the Dutch, as Noord-Wester Haven. Governor Adrian van der Stel, who governed between 1639 and 1645, began to introduce slaves from Madagascar to help the settlers with their agricultural and other work. Some of the slaves escaped almost as soon as they arrived and were a threat to the security of the colonists. This problem remained a serious one until slavery was eventually abolished in the nineteenth century. Sugar was introduced by the Dutch from Java and the settlers were constantly asking the authorities for more slave labour to help in the clearing and cultivation of the land. Fear of rebellion by runaway slaves, however, made the Company cautious about increasing the number of slaves too quickly.

Ebony

One task the early Dutch settlers carried out too successfully. This was the felling of ebony trees for their valuable timber. The first road to be built was from the forest near Flacq to Grand Port and its purpose was to make it easier to transport timber to the sea at Grand Port. As early as 1650 so much ebony had been exported that the price in Holland had fallen dramatically. Reynier Por, governor from 1648 to 1653, was ordered to restrict the felling of trees to 400 per year.

The Cape settlement

In 1652 the Dutch East India Company established another settlement at the Cape of Good Hope. Its main function was the same as that of Mauritius: to serve as a half-way station for Dutch ships on the long voyage to and from the East Indies and to supply fresh food and water for the ships. This new settlement was founded, as the settlement of Mauritius had been fourteen years earlier, from the fear that the English and French were about to do the same.

The Cape settlement made the one on Mauritius less important. By 1656 there were signs

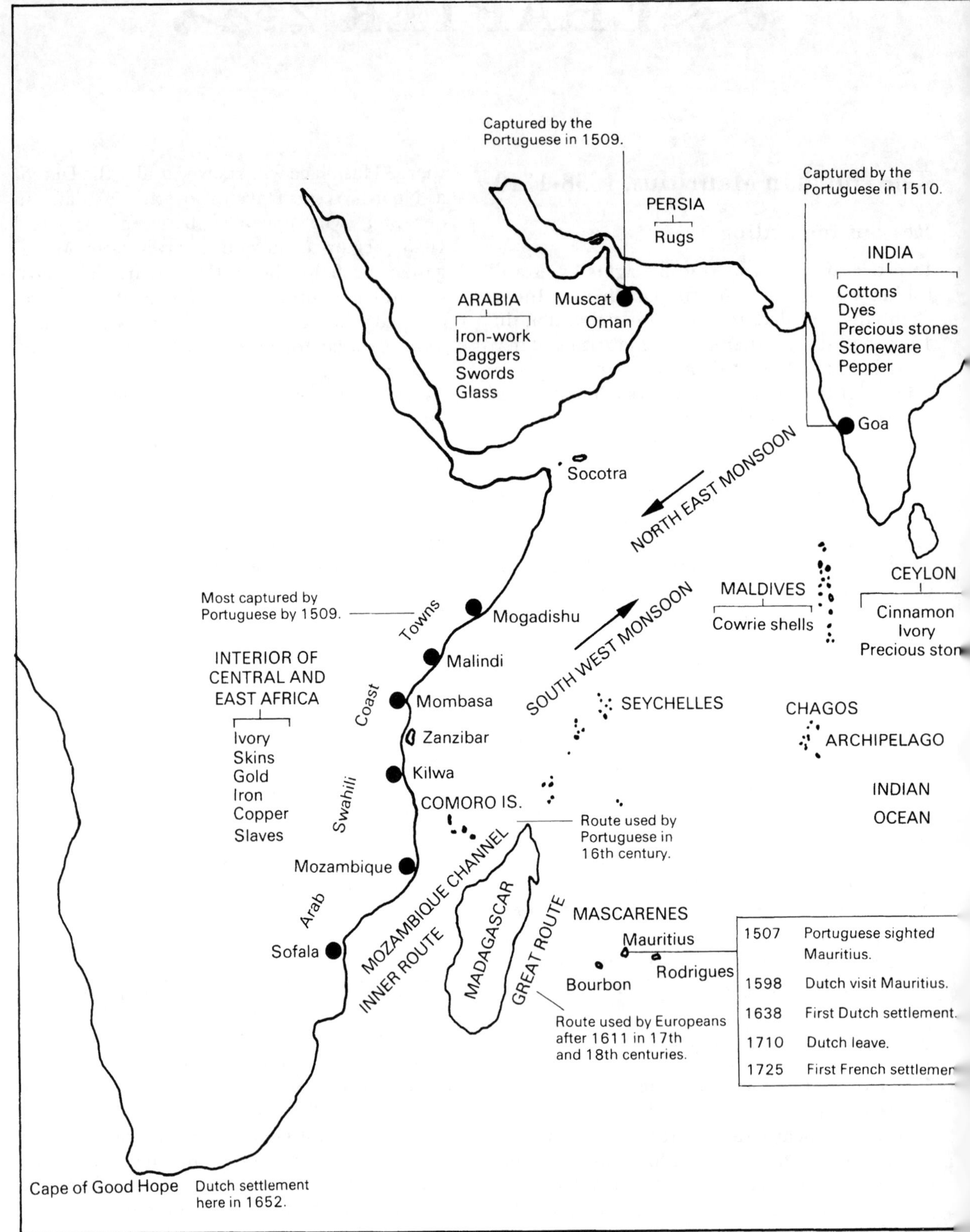

The trade of the Indian Ocean in medieval and early modern times

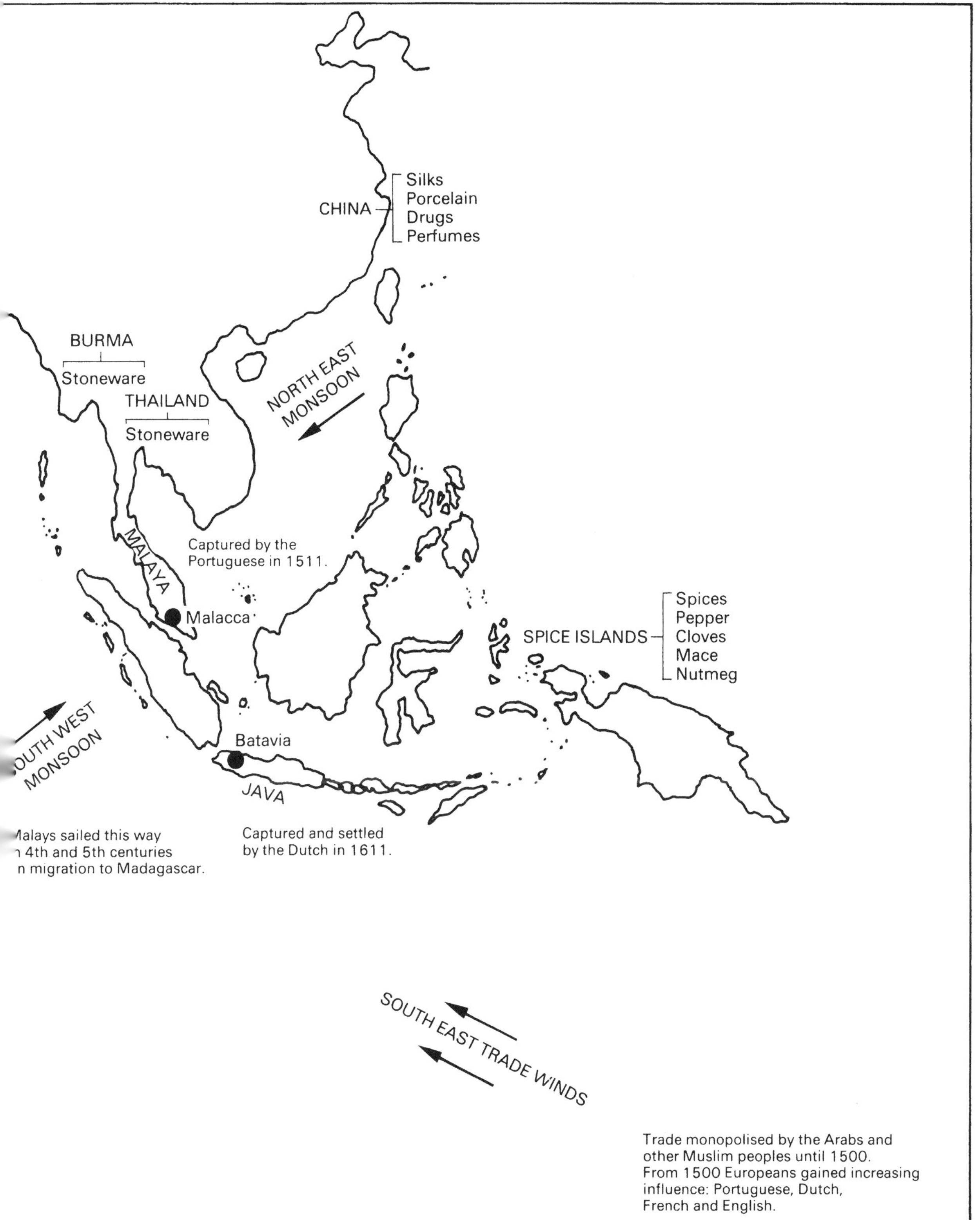
CHINA
Silks
Porcelain
Drugs
Perfumes
BURMA
Stoneware
THAILAND
Stoneware
NORTH EAST
MONSOON
MALAYA
Captured by the
Portuguese in 1511.
Malacca
SPICE ISLANDS
Spices
Pepper
Cloves
Mace
Nutmeg
Batavia
JAVA
OUTH WEST
MONSOON
Malays sailed this way
ı 4th and 5th centuries
n migration to Madagascar.
Captured and settled
by the Dutch in 1611.
SOUTH EAST TRADE WINDS
Trade monopolised by the Arabs and
other Muslim peoples until 1500.
From 1500 Europeans gained increasing
influence: Portuguese, Dutch,
French and English.

The dodo

that the Dutch East India Company was preparing to abandon Mauritius. They began to move some of their employees in Mauritius to the Cape and others to Batavia. In 1658 they left the island altogether after destroying anything that might be valuable to their rivals. They had introduced deer from Java to provide a supply of meat; they had cattle, some of which ran wild; less useful animals introduced by the Dutch were monkeys and rats. The island's famous flightless bird, the dodo, was quickly exterminated; its flesh was valuable food for the ships' crews.

The second settlement in Mauritius

In 1664, the Dutch returned. Perhaps they felt that, with the French and the English always liable to attack, two bases were always better than one. Perhaps they thought that, having done better at the Cape than in Mauritius, they might be more successful in Mauritius at the second attempt. They remained on the island for another forty-six years but never looked like establishing a really flourishing colony.

In 1673, after nearly ten years under three very mediocre governors, Nieuwland (1664-1665), Wreedon (1665-1672) and Telleson (1672-1673), the settlers sent a petition to the Cape asking that the settlement should be abandoned again. Instead they were sent a new governor, Hubert Hugo (1673-1677). He was an improvement on his predecessors and a number of achievements can be credited to his governorship. The few roads were improved; the fort was rebuilt and a sawmill was constructed. The settlers from Java, who had a reputation for being hard working, had begun to produce a variety of vegetables, pineapples and bananas and some rice. The Dutch, unfortunately, seem to have been less co-operative and Governor Hugo reported that gluttony had become a disease amongst them. They appear to have preferred to live on the readily available supplies of meat from the herds of deer and wild cattle on the island rather than exert themselves in growing crops and developing the island's resources.

Hugo's successor, Isaac Lamotius, was governor from 1677 to 1692, the longest period of rule by any of the island's governors. Lamotius was an autocrat who had little idea how to inspire the inhabitants, and the island was unhappy under his rule. It became normal for officials and settlers to stay for the minimum period of three years and to do as little work as possible during their stay. Lamotius was not equal to the task of controlling a community which contained too many bad characters and misfits. His troubles were increased when English pirates expelled from the Caribbean[1] began to arrive in the Indian Ocean and to use Mauritius as a base. He finally fell foul of his masters in the Dutch East India Company. He was suspected of befriending the English and was accused of ill-treating colonists and Company employees. A successor, Roelof Deodati, was appointed and his first duty was to arrest Lamotius and send him to Batavia, where he was tried and sentenced to six years' imprisonment.

The governorship of Deodati

Under Deodati, governor from 1692 to 1703, the pirate menace increased as more pirates were driven out of their old hunting grounds in the Caribbean after the Treaty of Ryswick in

1 *Caribbean: the islands and sea lying between North and South America and to the east of Central America. The islands are also called the West Indies.*

1697. Deodati was ruthless and unscrupulous in some of his actions and deliberately disobeyed some of the standing instructions to Dutch governors of the island.

In 1689 a group of ten French Huguenots[2], refugees from the persecution of Louis XIV, landed on the small island of Rodrigues. For a time they were happy on what seemed initially an island paradise. After nearly three years, however, they grew tired of their lonely life, they built themselves a boat and put to sea. Eight days later they were glad to put ashore on Mauritius where they were at first welcomed by the Dutch. Their undoing followed Deodati's discovery that they had amongst their meagre possessions a small quantity of ambergris. This was scarce and therefore very valuable and the governor and the islanders were under strict orders to send any ambergris they acquired back to Holland. Deodati wanted it for himself and seized it. He feared, however, that if the Frenchmen were allowed their freedom, they might report what he had done, so he exiled them to a small, barren island in Grand Port Bay where they were worse off than they had been on Rodrigues. A particularly violent cyclone hit Mauritius in February 1695 and further added to the problems of the small community.

It was under Deodati's successor as governor, Abraham van de Velde (1703-1710), that the Dutch finally abandoned the struggle to make a success of their Mauritius settlement. In 1710, after destroying all their buildings and stores, they withdrew either to the Cape or to Batavia.

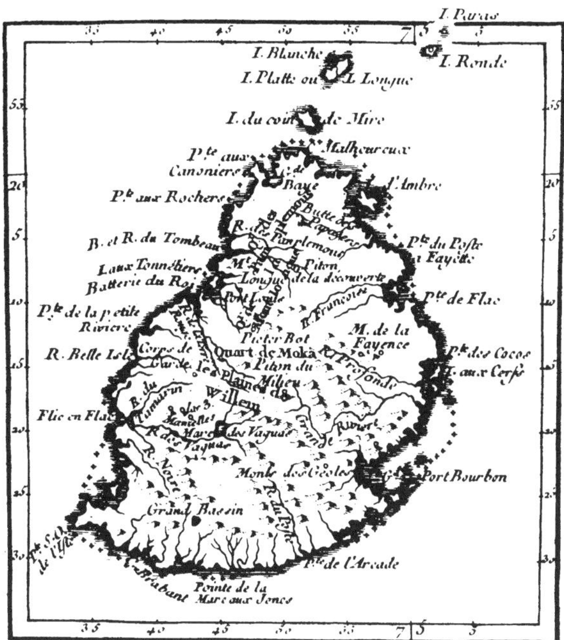

An early map of the Ile de France

Reasons for Dutch failure

The Dutch contribution to the history of Mauritius was not a very significant one. They gave the island the name which it retains today. They introduced, though hardly successfully established, sugar, the crop which eventually came to dominate its economy. They had exterminated the dodo and had practically denuded the island of its ebony. They left nothing behind which could make life easier for any inhabitants who might follow them.

The Dutch settlement in Mauritius was a failure; and although it is true that the crops which the Dutch planted were often destroyed by cyclones or drought or plagues of rats, these were not the main reasons for the failure. There were more serious causes. None of the Dutch governors was in any way distinguished. If Deodati was the most capable of them, the others must have been a bad lot. The absence of good leadership was undoubtedly one of the main reasons for the Dutch failure to colonise Mauritius.

Another reason for the failure was that the number of settlers and slaves was never large enough to establish a sound economic life based on agriculture. There were never more than about 400 people on the island. Any notion that Mauritius was at this time a tropical paradise should be forgotten. It had some fertile soil; but it was, on the whole, a harsh, rocky environment, large parts of it thickly wooded, which needed a lot of clearing and breaking in before it could be expected to support permanent inhabitants in a comfortable way of life.

The Dutch settlers, like their governors, seldom seem to have been the best of Dutch stock. They did not like hard work. When

2 *Huguenot: the name given to French Protestants from the sixteenth century. They were followers of John Calvin and were expelled from France by Louis XIV in 1685.*

crops were destroyed by cyclones, which were frequent, or by drought, as in 1707, or when meat supplies were suddenly cut down by the outbreak of disease amongst the island's livestock, they sat back and waited for supplies to be imported. Sometimes they had a long wait.

The Dutch community was also too predominantly male ever to become a contented and flourishing one. A few years before the settlement was abandoned there were one hundred and sixty-nine Dutch people and sixty-seven slaves on the island. Only fifty-eight of the Dutch were women. Toussaint goes so far as to claim that the Dutch failure 'can be largely accounted for by the lack of women colonists'.

If we ask why the Dutch abandoned Mauritius, we should remember the nature of the Dutch empire. The Dutch overseas empire was a commercial empire. Its purpose was to make profit through trade. Mauritius was becoming a liability rather than an asset. Its inhabitants were often unable to feed themselves, let alone supply passing Dutch ships and their crews with fresh meat and vegetables. Once the ebony had been exhausted Mauritius had little else of commercial value. Moreover, by the end of the seventeenth century the Dutch seemed prepared to abandon India, apart from Ceylon, captured from the Portuguese in 1658, to the English and the French. The Dutch East Indies was more than ever the most important part of their empire. They hardly needed both the Cape and Mauritius as a port of call for their ships on the way to the East Indies. If a choice had to be made the Cape was the more promising of the two settlements.

We can see now that, at the end of the seventeenth century, the balance of power in Europe was changing. The Dutch had passed the peak of their power and influence. Their great days lay in the first fifty or sixty years of the seventeenth century, when they won their independence from Spain, and when their rivals, France and England, were preoccupied with war and internal troubles. During those years, the Dutch enjoyed a remarkable period of success in trade, in industry, in science and in the arts. But this 'golden age' could hardly last for long. Dutch resources were too limited. There were not many more than one million Dutch. England and France were potentially much stronger and much richer.

Between 1651 and 1666 the Dutch fought three exhausting naval wars against the English, and from then until 1713 they fought a series of mainly land wars against the French. In the last of these, the War of the Spanish Succession with England as their ally, they were on the winning side. The English, however, took most of the spoils. More than half a century of almost continuous warfare had helped to weaken the tiny Dutch Republic. They had to learn to live at peace with their more powerful neighbours in the Indian Ocean as well as in Europe. They withdrew from Mauritius in 1710, shortly before the end of the war of the Spanish Succession. In the Indian Ocean, as in Europe, the Dutch had to content themselves with less ambitious plans than those of seventy years earlier when, in their period of greatness, they had first occupied Mauritius.

Suggestions for revision

You should know:

a) the reasons why the Dutch were interested in Mauritius;
b) about their activities and achievements on the island;
c) the reasons for the failure of their settlement and for their ultimate withdrawal.

Suggestions for further work

1 Think of reasons which may have led the Dutch to decide that their settlement at the Cape of Good Hope was more valuable to them than the one on Mauritius.
Why, after withdrawing from Mauritius in 1658, did they return again in 1664?
2 Several reasons are suggested in this chapter for the failure of the Dutch to make a successful settlement on Mauritius. Make a list of these. Which one do you consider to be the most important and why?
3 Find out more about the Dutch wars against England in the seventeenth century and the wars in which the Dutch fought as allies of England against the French later in the century. Why was the position of the Dutch slowly declining during this period?
4 Make sure you know the meaning of the following words: strategic, ambergris (page 5) and autocrat (page 8).

CHAPTER 3

The French in Mauritius
1 The East India Company, 1725-1767

The French were the last of the western European powers to enter the Indian Ocean to compete for its trade. In 1638, the year the Dutch began to settle in Mauritius, the French staked a claim to Réunion and Rodrigues. In 1642 the French Eastern Company, predecessor of the East India Company, sent an officer to set up a trading post on Madagascar. This was at Fort Dauphin on the south-east corner of the island. The officer also confirmed the earlier French claim to Réunion and Rodrigues and this was repeated in 1649. In that year the French named the larger of their two islands in the Mascarenes, Bourbon, a name it retained until 1814.

It was some time, however, before they made any serious attempt to establish a settlement on the island. They were not happy about Fort Dauphin. The local people were hostile and the base was insecure. For some time the French had thoughts of taking the Cape from the Dutch and establishing a base of their own a little further north at Saldanha Bay. But these came to nothing.

The settlement on Bourbon

In 1664 a Compagnie des Indes was established with the encouragement of Colbert, Louis XIV's great finance minister. One of its first activities was to send an expedition to make the first settlement on Bourbon in 1665. The main base was moved from St Paul's Bay to St Denis in 1669 but the settlement made little progress until 1676. In that year the settlers who had survived an attack by local people on the Madagascar base in 1674 were moved to Bourbon. This now became the French East India Company's main base in the Indian Ocean and the port of call for its ships on the voyage to the trading post at Pondicherry in India which had been acquired a few years earlier.

The colony grew slowly but at least with a little more promise than the Dutch settlement on Mauritius. When the Dutch withdrew from Mauritius in 1710 there were about 1000 people in Bourbon. Rather more than half of these were French and the balance between men and women was very nearly even. In this respect, as well as from the point of view of numbers, Bourbon was in a healthier and more promising state than Mauritius had been under the Dutch.

Bourbon, however, had one serious disadvantage. It possessed no good harbour and was therefore far from ideal either as a naval base or as a port for merchant ships. Mauritius was far superior. When it was abandoned by the Dutch in 1710 it became for the next few years, not surprisingly, a favourite base for the increasing number of pirates who had recently come into the Indian Ocean. No one liked pirates, least of all trading companies whose ships became their prey. The desire to control the pirates was one reason for the French interest in Mauritius.

French interest in Mauritius

In 1715 a sea captain, Dufresne d'Arsel, had called at Mauritius on a voyage from Mocha where his ship had picked up a cargo of coffee. He was one of a group of Breton merchants from St Malo who had become involved in two projects involving coffee. They were interested in trading in coffee between Mocha, in southern Arabia, and France. They were also trying to establish the cultivation of coffee on Bourbon. Attempts to grow other crops there, including cloves and pepper, had been tried and failed. Captain Dufresne was carrying the first coffee plants to Bourbon when he called at Mauritius, confirmed that it was unoccupied and claimed it for France under the name of the Ile de France. For the time being, however, he did

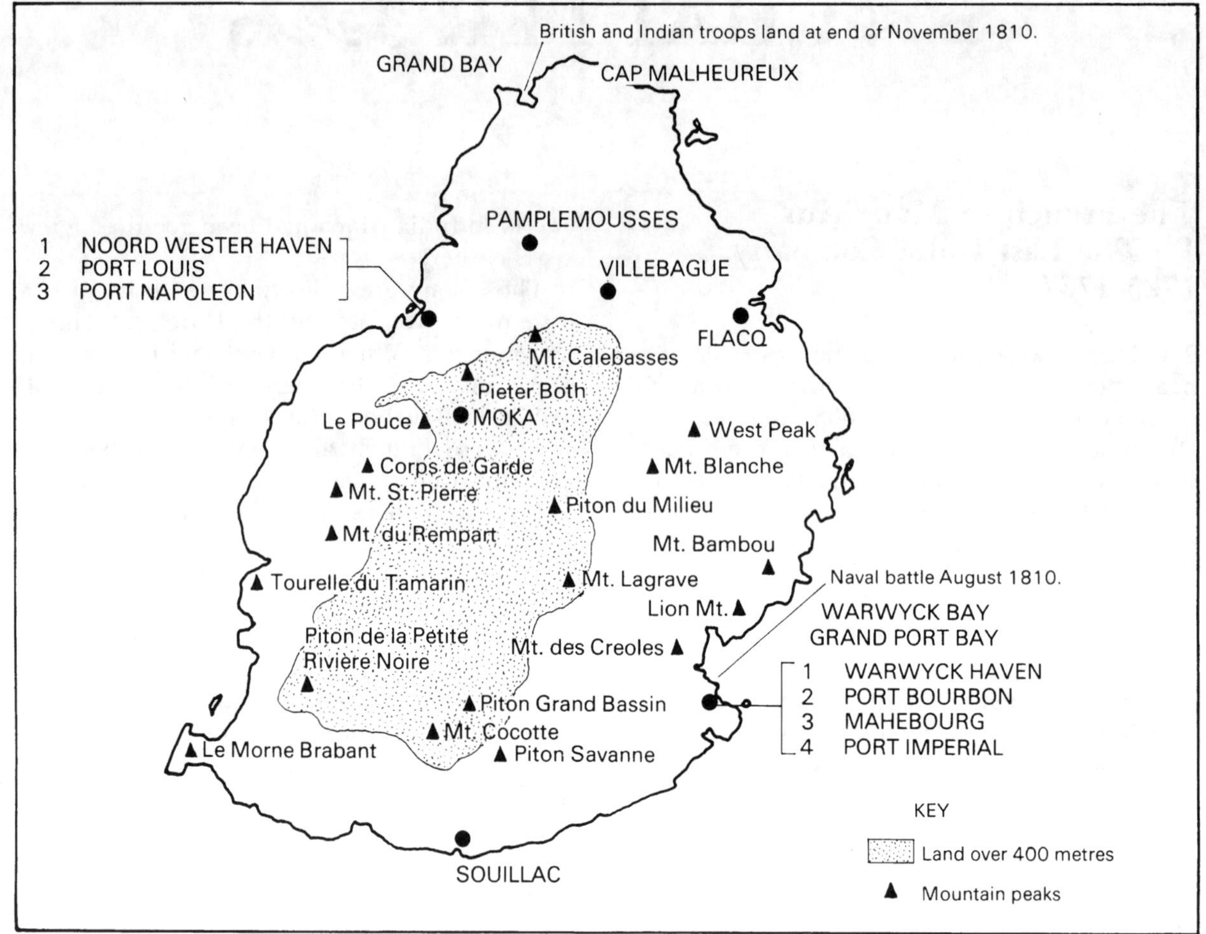

Mauritius under the Dutch and the French

not stay nor did he leave anyone else behind.

Within the next twenty years the growing of coffee was successfully established on Bourbon. The rate of growth was remarkable and exports rose from less than 20,000 pounds in 1725 to 2,500,000 pounds in 1744. The crop remained the basis of the island's economy for the next one hundred years. The main credit for this economic progress through coffee growing was due to Desforges-Boucher, who was firstly deputy governor and then governor between 1718 and 1725.

Early French settlers

It was while Desforges-Boucher was governor that the French began the settlement of the Ile de France. A small reconnaissance party was sent from Bourbon and landed at the north-west harbour, late in 1721. This was followed by a bigger party of settlers from France under the leadership of an engineer called Denyon. The two ports at opposite corners of the island were renamed. The former Noord-Wester Haven was called Port Louis. It is not certain whether this was in honour of Louis XV, then King of France, or after Port Louis in Brittany. Warwyck Haven was called Port Bourbon and Denyon favoured Port Bourbon as the main centre of government and the main port, as it had been under the Dutch.

Within three years differences of opinion about the choice of the island's capital, coupled with problems caused by unruly soldiers, destructive cyclones and large numbers of rats, left Denyon so discouraged and overwhelmed by the hopeless task facing him that he asked to be relieved of his job. His resignation coincided with the death of Desforges-Boucher in Bourbon and the man appointed to replace Denyon took over the governorship of Bourbon instead. The task of ruling the Ile de France fell to Monsieur de Brousse, commander of the garrison, who was not finally replaced by a civilian until 1729. There was a delay in setting up the provincial council or Conseil Supérieur which was to consist of six Company officials. This was finally established in 1726 but friction then developed between the Council and Monsieur de Brousse.

In 1727 the Company appointed a civilian, Pierre-Benoit Dumas, as governor of both islands. The main seat of power was to be in Bourbon but the governor was expected to spend three months out of every year in the Ile de France. However, the new system did not work, for Dumas was kept so busy in Bourbon that he was unable to spend part of each year in the Ile de France.

The tension between Monsieur de Brousse and the Council continued until 1729 when the Company gave the Ile de France its own administrator, Nicolas de Maupin. He was to be responsible to Dumas. Maupin was as pessimistic about the island's future prospects as Denyon had been but he did make one important decision. He recommended that Port Louis should become the main port and the centre of government. The Company considered Maupin's recommendation, and decided to send out an engineer to make a report on the relative merits of the two ports and to draw up plans for fortification. This man was named Cossigny. 'I would gladly pay a hundred thousand écus,' the manager told him, 'to know for a fact that it is possible to construct a harbour in the island in which ships will be safe from hurricanes.'

Cossigny left France at the end of 1731 and arrived in the Ile de France in June 1732. After making a survey of the ports he reached the conclusion that Port Louis would be the more suitable and he drew up plans to fortify the town and harbour. He then went to Bourbon where Governor Dumas asked him to join an expedition to Madagascar. Cossigny was a man who made enemies easily. He was said to have 'perfected quarrelling to a fine art'. On this expedition he fell out with Dumas and soon afterwards with almost every official of the Company and every member of the Council. In 1734 Cossigny learned that the Company approved of his proposals and wanted him to carry them out at once.

On his return to the Ile de France, he could not get the work started, partly because he himself would be content with nothing short of perfection and partly because he was short of suitable workers, equipment and materials. The Company's officials were uninterested in his scheme. He complained about the laziness of the workers and antagonised them by his autocratic methods. The situation became impossible and Cossigny's presence was an obstacle to progress. The Council decided that he must go and ordered him to leave. He left for France early in 1735.

The governorship of Labourdonnais

A few months later a new governor arrived to take charge in the Ile de France. This was Bertrand Francois Mahé de Labourdonnais. He was without doubt the greatest of all the governors of the islands. When he arrived in 1735 there were still doubts about the permanence of the French settlement. When he

The statue of Mahé de Labourdonnais at Port Louis

left eleven years later the colony was firmly established. In 1735 there was little sign of any development of either the harbour or the town at Port Louis; by 1746 the harbour was well-equipped and well-defended and the town was a flourishing place with some fine buildings, a social life and the air of a capital in the making.

Early career

Like so many of the French who helped to put the Ile de France on its feet, Labourdonnais was a Breton, born in St Malo. He was only thirty-six when he arrived in the Ile de France but already he had a breadth of experience and a list of achievements which fitted him well for his post. He went to sea at the age of ten and first saw the Indian Ocean, scene of his greatest achievements, when he was fourteen. He served with the French East India Company but also set up as a trader on his own.

By 1732 there were few places in the Indian Ocean which Labourdonnais had not visited on his trading voyages. He had also made personal acquaintances of many rulers and people in positions of importance. In 1732 whilst in Pondicherry he heard from his brother, who was a member of the Council there, that the governorship of the Ile de France would soon be vacant. He returned to France to press his claim to the post. He made an influential marriage which made him known to two brothers who would wield enormous influence in the appointment to the post he was seeking; Orvy de Fulvy, who was Inspector General of the East India Company, and Jean Henri Orvy, Controller General of Finance. They had already played an important part in Cossigny's appointment several years earlier and Cossigny was now one of the candidates for the post of governor.

Labourdonnais' connection through marriage no doubt counted in his favour. More important, however, were a number of critical reports he had written on the waste and inefficiency in Company administration in general and the corruption and malpractices in the government of Pondicherry. In submitting such reports at this time, he was taking a gamble, but it paid off. The Orvy brothers and the Company directors recognised that Labourdonnais possessed the qualities they were looking for in the new governor. He was appointed in November 1734.

Labourdonnais was a man of tireless energy and considerable vision. He worked hard and expected hard work from others and was not universally popular. Few men can have had as full an understanding as he had of the commercial and strategic position of the Ile de France in the Indian Ocean, or as clear a picture of its importance in the struggle already beginning between his own country and Britain. He saw his role in the island, or rather in the Mascarenes as a whole, to consist of two tasks. One was to satisfy the immediate needs and interests of the islands and develop them into permanent and flourishing colonies; the other was to use their resources to meet the demands imposed by the broader strategic needs of France in the coming struggle for power.

Plans for extending French influence in the Indian Ocean

Bourbon, with its coffee growing already a thriving business, was in 1735 more securely placed than the Ile de France. Labourdonnais planned to develop Bourbon as an agricultural community. The Ile de France was to be developed as the site of a commercial port and strategic naval base. Labourdonnais started a shipyard, so that ships could actually be built and not merely repaired at Port Louis. But he realised that these commercial and naval facilities could not be provided unless there were a flourishing community in Port Louis and a well-developed economic life on the island as a whole, capable at least of supplying the inhabitants with their food.

It was, perhaps, in his plan for promoting France's interests in the Indian Ocean as a whole that Labourdonnais can be seen at his greatest. The story of his part in the wars between 1740 and 1748 is described in Chapter 7. His grand design for the extension of French influence in the Ocean was not, however, accepted in its entirety either by the government at home or by the French East India Company. He was anxious that the French should take possession of a substantial part of Mozambique on the African mainland, where the Portuguese were already established. They did not do so; but in his time an increasing number of the slaves used in the Ile de France were recruited in Mozambique rather than in Madagascar. He had little interest in Madagascar itself but a great deal of interest in the various groups of islands to the north and east of the Mascarenes. It was one of his officers, Captain Picault, who first explored these islands systematically in 1742, claimed them for France as an annexe of the Ile de France and named them the Mahé islands after Labourdonnais. In 1756 they were renamed the Seychelles in honour of Moreau de Séchelles who was then Secretary of the Navy in France.

In two other respects Labourdonnais' plan for the Ile de France in the Indian Ocean bore fruit in the future rather than in his own days. He was in favour of using the island as a base for commerce raiders as well as for a naval squadron. Perhaps he realised that Britain's position in the Indian Ocean was too strong to be shaken, and felt that commerce raiding might be a more effective way of harming France's enemy than direct naval action. It would also have been a way of using the talent and energy of the many pirates in the area in the semi-official capacity of licensed corsairs. As we shall see, the activities of the corsairs later in the eighteenth century and on into the Napoleonic Wars became a serious threat to British shipping. In Labourdonnais' time, however, the East India Company rejected his proposals for commerce raiding.

Labourdonnais did have his way temporarily over another issue. He believed that the island would benefit if its trading facilities were opened up to all traders. He wanted Port Louis to be made into a free port. This meant the abandonment by the East India Company of its monopoly of trade. Reluctantly, the Company agreed from 1742 to 1747. The results were disappointing, however, and the arrangements ended soon after Labourdonnais' departure. It was revived with much more beneficial results for the island's economy under Governor Farquhar, the first of the British governors.

Building the harbour at Port Louis

On his arrival as governor in 1735, one of Labourdonnais' first decisions was to move the main administrative headquarters from Bourbon to the Ile de France. Labourdonnais' first task was to implement the plans for the construction of the harbour and fortifications at Port Louis, drawn up by Cossigny, but left virtually unstarted.

Labourdonnais was well aware of some of the problems and came with ready-made solutions to some of them and plans for dealing with others. He brought with him qualified architects and other workmen from Madras with the necessary skills for the job. Strict regulations were laid down governing hours and conditions of work. Contracts were made with local suppliers to try to ensure that the necessary materials were obtained. Dock workers and sailors were brought in from Pondicherry and other French trading stations in India. The work went ahead smoothly and Cossigny returned in 1736 to find that Labourdonnais had succeeded where he himself had failed. By 1740 Port Louis had a well-constructed harbour run by a harbour department staffed with a variety of skilled men.

In building the harbour Labourdonnais did not neglect the supporting services of the port as a commercial centre and a naval base nor the needs of the increasing number of inhabitants of the town, now the capital of the Mascarenes. Amongst the former were warehouses, a dry dock, an armoury and powder magazine, barracks and a fort, La Redoute Labourdonnais. Amongst the facilities for the people in general was an aqueduct which brought a good fresh water supply over three miles from Grand River North-West, and a hospital which he visited personally each day for over a year to check that it was running efficiently. Port Louis was also graced with a few buildings which befitted what had just become a capital and centre of administration. A Government House was built and an official residence for the governor, 'Monplaisir'. The latter was at Pamplemousses and stood in its own grounds which have since become one of the world's best-known botanic gardens.

New crops

In these gardens at Pamplemousses, Labourdonnais experimented in the growing of new crops, an interest which had a very practical purpose. Since the first Dutch settlement was made on Mauritius in 1638, one of the main obstacles to the establishment of a permanent settlement had been the precarious nature of

A view of Pamplemousses in 1828

the island's food supplies. Cyclones often destroyed crops and left the inhabitants totally dependent on imported food. Labourdonnais tried hard to improve this unsatisfactory state of affairs. He gave every encouragement to agriculture and particularly to the growing of food crops. His greatest success, acknowledged by Cossigny who was no friend of Labourdonnais, was the introduction of manioc or cassava which was brought from Brazil. The island's climate was ideal for its cultivation, it needed only a short growing season and it stood up well to the frequent cyclones. Sugar cultivation spread slowly and the island's first sugar factory was built by Labourdonnais' brother at Villebague. Other crops grown included maize and other cereals, potatoes and other vegetables, rice on a small scale and cotton and indigo.

The population increased within the first four years of Labourdonnais' governorship from just under 1000 to over 3000. The food supply was still not secure or reliable, but it was in a healthier state than ever before. The island's capacity for producing food was often overstretched within the next twenty years by the presence of large numbers of sailors and soldiers on their way to and from the fighting between England and France in India (see Chapter 7). Occasionally these temporary visitors outnumbered the permanent residents and found themselves unpopular.

Establishing order

Labourdonnais' third contribution to the history of Mauritius was the establishment of internal order. The great threat to the peace and security of the colonists came from the large numbers of runaway slaves hiding away in the interior of the island. Much of the countryside was densely wooded and provided ideal conditions for these runaways. They were desperate men who feared the consequences of recapture and would stop at nothing to avoid being caught. Just before Labourdonnais' arrival, attacks on isolated farms were frequent There were even cases where runaway slaves murdered colonists on the outskirts of Port Louis.

Labourdonnais tackled this problem as he did others, with more energy and more systematically than his predecessors. He organised what seemed to be an early example of a campaign against terrorist tactics. Part of the island's garrison was given the special task of patrolling the forests to track down the runaways. Men with experience and skill as hunters were enlisted to train the soldiers in forest warfare. The efforts of the regular soldiers were supplemented by a detachment of irregular troops recruited from amongst the slaves. The menace of the runaways was not entirely stamped out but it was greatly reduced before the end of Labourdonnais' governorship. Islanders were able to travel more safely on the more numerous and better-built roads which were another part of Labourdonnais' legacy to the Ile de France. Pamplemousses and Moka were both linked to Port Louis by road.

Since Labourdonnais left in 1746, Mauritius has faced many problems and weathered many crises. But its continued existence and growth has never again been in serious doubt, as it was when Labourdonnais arrived in 1735. His name is more widely known today than that of any other figure in the early history of the island and he is still commemorated in several ways.

Le Réduit

The final years of Company rule

The island remained under Company rule for twenty years after Labourdonnais left. For much of that time its development and the life of its inhabitants were affected by the wars between France and England. Even when, officially, there was peace in Europe, the rivalry and the spasmodic fighting continued in India and the Indian Ocean and also in North America.

In this period the Ile de France had four more governors. It should be remembered that they were governors of the Mascarenes and that their headquarters were now on the Ile de France. None of these four governors possessed the vision of Labourdonnais and none had his experience and understanding of the general position in the Indian Ocean. They were anxious to concentrate on the local needs and interests of the Ile de France and resented the demands placed on the island's limited resources by the strategic importance it had acquired in the Indian Ocean. There is no doubt that their efforts to improve agriculture were frustrated and undermined by these demands, especially during the Seven Years' War (1756-1763).

Félix Barthélemy David (1746-1751) was Labourdonnais' immediate successor. He built a new residence for himself near Moka, Le Réduit. This became the favourite residence of the governors but the cost of building it was an expense that the Company could ill afford. But the war of the Austrian Succession[1] ended in 1748 and the Company, with some relief, was able to order its governor to concentrate on food production.

David's successor was Charles Lozier-Bouvet (1751-1755). During his governorship Cossigny returned to the Ile de France to continue the building of the fortifications at Port Louis. Before he had been back for long he had quarrelled with the governor and many others whose co-operation was essential to the progress of his work. The governor requested his recall but this was not granted. By 1756 it was Cossigny himself who asked to be sent home. Again he was told to stay and continue the work on the defences. The work was also held up by two serious outbreaks of smallpox and Cossigny finally left in 1759 with his task still unfinished.

Lozier-Bouvet gave some of his time to the problems created by the presence of large numbers of slaves. In spite of Labourdonnais' efforts to solve it, the problem of escaped slaves continued. Lozier-Bouvet began keeping records of the island's slaves and started a register of slaves and their masters. It was a step towards closer control and supervision of the slaves.

His governorship was a period of peace and he gave encouragement and practical assistance to a Company agent, Pierre Poivre, who

1 *War of the Austrian Succession: a war principally between Austria and Prussia but involving several of the European powers including Britain, on the side of Austria, and France, on the side of Prussia.*

was interested in establishing the cultivation of spices on the island. Lozier-Bouvet provided Poivre with a ship in which he made a voyage to the Dutch East Indies. He brought back a variety of spice plants but they were never cultivated on a large scale; but Poivre himself was to play an important part in the island's history before long (see Chapter 4).

The effect of the Seven Years' War

The beginning of René Magon's governorship coincided with the beginning of the Seven Years' War. It was he who had to try to cope with the massive problem posed for the island by the arrival of Lally-Tollendal's and Admiral d'Aché's major expedition (see Chapter 7). Magon had a real interest in agriculture and eventually, in 1759, asked to be relieved of the impossible task of supplying the needs of the expedition. His request was granted.

It was a pity that Magon was not given an opportunity to follow his real interests. He was one of the earliest rulers, along with Labourdonnais, who believed that the island's best hope of a successful economy lay in the cultivation of sugar cane. He purchased the sugar plantation at Villebague, the first of any size on the island, built himself a new house on the estate and retired there after he had been relieved of his governorship. He also tried to encourage meat products by importing cattle from Madagascar, but all that the island could produce was swallowed up by the soldiers and sailors.

Antoine-Marie Desforges-Boucher (1759-1767) was the last of the Company governors. Magon's last task had been to try to provision, repair and restore to fighting order d'Aché's battered and dispirited force. D'Aché put to sea but returned again in November 1759 to face the new governor with the same problems. Desforges-Boucher faced the situation realistically. The island's stocks were exhausted and it was incapable of supporting d'Aché's men. A cyclone in 1760 destroyed most of the growing crops and made an already difficult situation into a hopeless one. Desforges-Boucher had no alternative but to order d'Aché and his ships to leave as soon as possible.

In fact the Seven Years' War had shown that there were limitations to what the Ile de France could be expected to do in refitting and provisioning a fleet for a major war at this time. It was too far from the main scene of the fighting. Apart from this, however, its resources in terms of food and proper accommodation were inadequate for a large expedition such as that which had descended on it several times between 1757 and 1759.

Some lessons were learned from the problems of these years. One of Desforges-Boucher's main undertakings was to construct extensive barracks as quarters for visiting troops and garrisons. Most of the soldiers and sailors had been billeted in private houses with disastrous consequences for discipline and good relations between the troops and the inhabitants.

Another different development of these years was an equally interesting response to the military and naval situation during the Seven Years' War. From the point of view of France, the French East India Company and the people of the Ile de France, the Seven Years' War was a disaster. Defeated in North America and in India, the French lost most of their overseas possessions. The Company's trade with India had slumped and its profits had suffered. As for the islanders, their lives had been disrupted and their very survival threatened. It was not the strength of the French fleet that had saved them from attack but Britain's interest in more important targets. In self-defence and as a means of retaliation and livelihood many of the male inhabitants turned to privateering. They become corsairs; commerce raiders, licensed by the authorities to attack enemy ships. There was an important distinction between corsairs and pirates and this was that the former had official permission to plunder the ships of enemy nations whereas pirates attacked any worthwhile ship of any country. The profession of the corsair became an important and an honourable one on the Ile de France until the island was captured by the British in 1810.

In the meantime the Seven Years' War had so seriously affected the fortunes of the East India Company that it was forced to sell the Ile de France to the French Crown. The transaction took place in 1764 and the price paid was twelve million pounds. It was not until 1767, however, that royal administration was established on the island and the Company's rule was ended.

Suggestions for revision

You should know:

a) the story of early French settlement and activity before the arrival of Labourdonnais in 1735;
b) the main facts about the work and achievements of Labourdonnais, both in the Ile de France and in the wider sphere of the Indian Ocean and the struggle between England and France during the War of the Austrian Succession, 1740-1748 (see also Chapter 7);
c) the main achievements of the French during the period of East India Company rule (1725-1767) and also the reasons for the handing over of control to the Crown;
d) the system of government and administration in the Ile de France and the Mascarenes under the East India Company.

Suggestions for further work

1 Make a list of the advantages and disadvantages of a) Bourbon and b) the Ile de France as settlements and bases for the French in the Indian Ocean before 1735.

2 In what ways did Labourdonnais' early career make him well qualified to become governor of the Mascarenes in 1735?

3 a) What benefits and b) what disadvantages did the close involvement in the struggle between Britain and France in the Indian Ocean bring to the Ile de France and its inhabitants?

4 Make sure you know the meaning of the following words: reconnaissance (page 12), manioc (cassava) and indigo (page 16).

CHAPTER 4

The French in Mauritius
2 Royal administration, 1767-1790

System of government

For just over twenty years between 1767 and the outbreak of revolution in France, the Ile de France was a crown colony governed by a royal governor and an intendant.[1] Of these two officials the governor theoretically held supreme authority. In practice, however, the personality and character of the two men often decided their relative power in the government of the island. To some extent there was a division of responsibility between the two. The governor exercised military and naval authority and a general supervision of civil government. The intendant was in charge of finance and justice. It was often difficult, however, to lay down dividing lines between their respective areas and the intendant particularly could wield enormous authority through his control of finance. In a period when construction work both on the harbour and on the fortifications of Port Louis continued to take up a lot of time, the engineers in charge of such work were also important figures in the Ile de France.

The old 'Conseils Supérieurs' (there had been one for Bourbon and one for the Ile de France) lapsed with the end of Company rule and the new councils were little more than courts of justice. The island was subdivided into districts, the number of which changed from eight to eleven and then finally to nine during the period of royal administration. Each district commandant was responsible to the governor and to the intendant.

When the period of royal government began, the island soon learned the political dangers of a system under which power was shared by two leading officials on a lonely island several months' journey away from the government that had appointed them. The first royal governor was Daniel Dumas and the intendant was Pierre Poivre, the agent of the East India Company who had introduced spices into the Ile de France from the Moluccas some twenty years earlier. To work efficiently the system of government required these two officials to co-operate; but they quarrelled from the start. The situation was resolved after about sixteen months; Dumas was recalled and Poivre, who was found guilty of insubordination to his superior officer, was reprimanded.

Pierre Poivre

1 *intendant: an important official of the French monarchy originating in the seventeenth century and lasting until the French Revolution. An intendant represented the King in every province and exercised wide powers, especially in the fields of finance and justice.*

Equally serious differences existed between Desroches, Dumas' successor, and Poivre, at least over the agricultural development of the island. Poivre was keen to make the Ile de France and Bourbon into spice growing islands. Desroches, more reasonably, was in favour of the production of more basic food crops. In other respects, however, the two men agreed well enough on the main priorities and a great deal of essential work of reconstruction was carried out before both retired at the same time in 1772.

The development of Port Louis

There was much in Port Louis that required urgent attention after the lean years of Company rule. A good deal of the pioneering work of Labourdonnais had suffered from neglect and shortage of funds. The harbour was silting up and was seriously obstructed by the wrecks of ships sunk by cyclones. The defences and many of the main buildings were in a bad state of repair. In spite of the work of Desforges-Boucher, accommodation for residents and visiting soldiers and sailors was still inadequate. The road network was in need of extension. In all these respects the restoration work or new construction which Desroches and Poivre carried out greatly improved the facilities and the appearance of the capital. They tried to insist that only stone houses should be erected inside the town and that streets should be paved with cobbles. Some of their buildings and some of their streets survive today.

They also were at one in trying to raise the moral standards of the town. They were anxious to build a town where respectable people could live happily. Many of the inhabitants of the town and the countryside were honest and respectable people. It was a period when the numbers of well-to-do people increased. Gracious living was established in well-built, well-furnished homes scattered throughout the island. Social occasions were held more frequently and men and women were dressed fashionably.

There were, however, far too many undesirables living on the island: men who had deserted or been turned out of the army or navy; fortune hunters who had come out from France expecting to get rich quickly and did not care whether they did so by honest or dishonest means. Desroches reported: 'Many businessmen made money so dishonestly that they hurried back at once to France, rather than remain on an island where everyone knew how dishonestly they had acquired their riches'. The two officials believed that drunkenness was too common. They closed down the cheap drinking houses and left only about twelve inns. Unfortunately the liquor served at these establishments was so weak that many illegal houses sprang up serving potent local drinks, mainly made from sugar cane. Desroches and Poivre issued a spate of edicts and though these were not all obeyed at least the two officials could not be accused of indifference or inactivity.

Poivre's achievements

Poivre was the more able of the two men. Indeed, apart from Labourdonnais, he was almost certainly the greatest of all the French officials to serve in the Ile de France. Toussaint lists the following as his main contributions to Port Louis: three water mills, each able to produce 6000 pounds of flour a day; a bakery able to provide enough bread for the garrison and also for provisioning ships; and new warehouses containing a reserve stock of 400,000 pounds of wheat, 400,000 of flour and 150,000 of rice. Besides this, he improved the harbour facilities and organised an engineering service, which had been almost non-existent in 1767. Finally, the town of Port Louis had grown by one-third and he had provided it with two essentials: a printing works, which began work in 1768, and a pharmacy.

Administration 1772-1789

Desroches and Poivre were replaced by Charles Louis de Ternay (1772-1776) and Maillart Dumesle (1772-1777). Like their predecessors they issued many decrees. Amongst these were orders regulating the sale of liquor and limiting the number of drinking houses and another forbidding the construction of new wooden houses in the town, problems already tackled, but obviously not solved, by edicts in the time of Desroches and Poivre. Much the same activities seem to have occupied the attention of the various governors and intendants until the beginning of the Revolution in 1789. They were matters that were bound to be the perennial concern of those responsible for the government of an expanding community such as Port Louis and the Ile de France then were: road building; provision for markets; general building, construction and improvement of urban facilities. The governors were La Brillane (1776-1779), the Vicomte François de Souillac (1779-1787), Raymond d'Entrecasteaux (1787-1789) and Thomas Conway (1789-1790) who was in the Ile de France when news of the Revolution reached the island. The intendants were Foucault (1777-1781), Chevreau (1781-1785), Narbonne (1785-1789) and Dupuy. Occasionally less routine activities were undertaken. At the beginning of their period of office in 1772, Ternay and Dumesle conducted a census in Port Louis. In 1779 Souillac decreed that whites were not to live in districts reserved for blacks. Clearly this implied that in theory a policy of residential segregation was being attempted by the authorities in Port Louis but that it was not being observed.

Under Governor Souillac the social life of the island blossomed, even though his governship coincided with another outbreak of warfare between France and Britain. This developed from Britain's war with her American colonists. In 1778 the French intervened on the side of the colonists, seizing the opportunity to avenge themselves for their defeat in the Seven Years' War. The great French admiral Suffren was in charge of the French fleet in the Indian Ocean. After visiting the island Suffren was reluctant to return to the Ile de France. He believed that the gay social life of the island was demoralising for his men. For the settlers and their ladies it was a welcome distraction from some of the harsher realities of everyday life.

New prosperity and improvements

The war of 1778 to 1783 provided further proof of the prosperity of the island, and the economic progress it had made since the Seven Years' War. Then the visit of Lally-Tollendal and d'Aché and their troops had proved too much for the island's resources. Twenty years later the position was different. Vessels came and went with troops on their way to and from India. Suffren's fleet alone had 11,000 men. Well over one hundred warships called at Port Louis in the last three years of the war. All these ships and men were adequately accommodated and were supplied with the weapons, ammunition and food they required. It was no fault of the Ile de France if the French were again defeated in India.

The Ile de France was able to cope with the problems brought by the war of 1778 to 1783,

Admiral Suffren's arrival at Mauritius in 1783

whereas it had failed to do so between 1756 and 1763, because, since the beginning of the royal administration, its economy had grown so well. One of the principal causes of growth was the freeing of the island's trade by the ending of the East India Company's monopoly in 1770. The steady increase in the number of ships visiting the island was one sign of growing prosperity. In 1769, the last year before free trade was permitted, seventy-eight ships visited Port Louis. In 1773 there were one hundred and three; in 1783, one hundred and seventy-six; in 1789, two hundred and three and in 1803, three hundred and forty-seven. A good many of the new trading ships came from the recently independent United States of America. The Ile de France's own merchants were amongst those who benefited from the new situation. They traded especially with other ports around the Indian Ocean; with Madagascar and the Portuguese ports on the East African coast for slaves; with Mocha and Muscat; with French and British ports in India and with the Dutch East Indies. A new French company was founded in 1785 but the old monopoly was not restored.

Agriculture

Several of the officials in this period tried to develop the island's agriculture but it is not entirely clear to what extent they succeeded. Poivre's ambition to establish the cultivation of spices, including cloves and nutmegs, on a commercial scale, was certainly not realised. Cultivation of sugar cane spread, especially during the war years, 1778 to 1783. By 1786 there were ten sugar factories on the island. However, conditions were still not ripe for a rapid expansion. Consumption of sugar on the island was low and Europe's needs were easily met by the Caribbean growers. Much of the cane was used in the manufacture of spirits. Indigo was another crop that was grown at this time, but its quality could not rival that of indigo grown in India. It was probably in the growth of food crops that the main expansion in agriculture took place. Even so some food was still imported, most of it from Madagascar and Bourbon.

Commerce and commerce raiding

Commerce raiding by corsairs continued to be another major economic activity. About thirty ships operated as commerce raiders against British merchant ships passing between India and the Cape. The Pitot family, Dubignon, Deschiens de Kerulvay and Chandeuil were amongst the most famous of the corsairs in this period and they captured booty worth several million francs.

Harbour improvements

Improvements to the harbour also helped the authorities to handle the many ships using the port during the war. These were the work of a naval engineer, the Chevalier de Tromelin, who rescued the harbour from the almost unusable condition it was in at the end of the period of the East India Company's rule. Tromelin arrived in Port Louis in 1768 and had prepared his plan for the harbour within two years. The plan was in two parts. The existing harbour needed to be cleared of the wrecks which all but blocked it and then cleared of silt by dredging. Future silting was prevented by the diversion of the streams which had brought down the silt. In addition to this clearing operation Tromelin planned a double extension, one on each side of the original harbour. On the east side the bay known as the Trou Fanfaron was to be converted into a harbour big enough to hold large naval vessels and several smaller ones. This improvement was carried out between 1772 and 1781 and was used to provide accommodation for naval vessels during the war. Work was temporarily halted when Tromelin left the Ile de France in 1781. It was finally completed in 1789, along with the building of a new arsenal. The final part of the plan, the construction of another extension on the Caudan side to the west, was not carried out during this period. Without Tromelin's work on the harbour Port Louis could not have served as a base for French naval operations in India during the American War of Independence.

General prosperity of the period

In spite of the printing of too much paper money which affected the stability of the island's currency and of periodic setbacks caused by the ravages of cyclones and defeat in war, the years of royal government were, on the whole, years of considerable growth. The

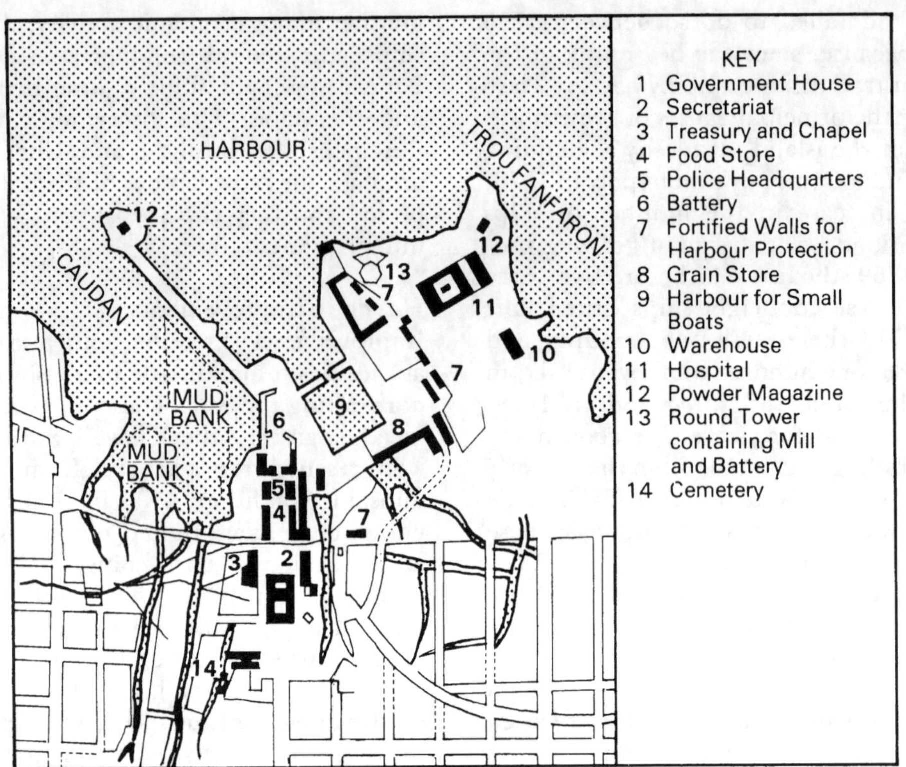

Port Louis and the harbour towards the end of the East India Company's rule in 1759

population of the island at the beginning and the end of this period is a measure of this. In 1766 there were about 20,000 inhabitants. Of these just under 2000 were white or 'freemen' and about 18,000 were slaves. In 1788 the figures had risen to nearly 43,000; 7000 free and 36,000 slaves. The total population had more than doubled and the number of whites and freemen had more than trebled in just over twenty years.

The slave population

Any claim about the years of royal government being a period of economic growth must not be allowed to hide the fact that, as is shown by the figures in the previous paragraph, over four-fifths of the population of the island were slaves who can have had no share in any increased prosperity.

Since the early days of French settlement slaves had been constantly brought to the island to provide its main labour force. Initially most came from Madagascar. From the late 1720s an increasing number were brought from West Africa, mainly from the East India Company's base at Goree off Senegal. Labourdonnais favoured the East African coast which had the advantage of being much closer. Smaller numbers of slaves also came from parts of Asia, mainly from India and Malaya. By the beginning of the period of royal government slavery was already a central part of the way of life of the island.

Some leading officials including Poivre and Ternay publicly lamented the fact that this was so. Ternay blamed the Company for introducing the practice of slave labour. In his opinion and that of other officials it would have been better if the French had relied, as they had done in their North American colony of Quebec, on small peasant cultivators. For a variety of reasons it had turned out differently on the Ile de France. The climate was one of the main reasons. Another was the need for a large number of manual workers to do the hard work of clearing the rock-strewn land for the cultivation of crops. The number of slaves had exceeded the number of free inhabitants from the start. The five to one ratio of slaves to whites and freemen was soon established and this was maintained until slavery was abolished in the 1830s.

It has been claimed by some writers that the slaves on the Ile de France lived and worked under more favourable conditions than those in other places where slavery was widely practised. The evidence for this claim, however, is not entirely convincing. It rests partly on the existence of laws which, in theory, gave some protection to slaves. Collectively these laws were known as the *Code Noir*. Certainly some new laws were introduced in the period of royal administration in an attempt to regulate the conditions of slaves. In 1767, for example, under Dumas and Poivre, a decree laid down that masters had to provide their slaves with two pounds of maize, or its equivalent, daily and with adequate clothing annually. Slaves had the right, theoretically, to complain to the Procureur Général if their entitlement to food and clothing was not met by their masters. It is difficult to believe, however, that illiterate slaves would be aware of such rights and even more difficult to imagine that they would dare to lodge complaints against their masters. In 1762 the office of Syndic was created. The duty of the Syndic was to protect slaves against ill-treatment and exploitation. It is unlikely, however, that the Syndic carried out his duties in this respect any more effectively than the Protector of Immigrants did in relation to Indian indentured labourers in the nineteenth century (see Chapter 10).

The writings of Rose de Freycinet, a French lady who visited the island early in the nineteenth century, are also quoted as evidence of the better conditions of slaves in Mauritius. She wrote that she had been assured that the negroes on the island were treated with greater kindness than those in other places and that she had heard Europeans in Mauritius argue that most peasants in France were less happy than the island's slaves. She was, however, reporting what she had been told rather than what she had seen for herself; and her informants were European inhabitants who were almost certainly slave owners themselves and, therefore, hardly reliable informants. What we do know from abundant evidence throughout the eighteenth century is that the problem of escaped slaves or 'marrons' was a permanent one which the authorities failed to solve. It had previously been a problem for the Dutch (see Chapter 2); but, because of the much larger numbers involved, it became a more serious one for the French. Its continued existence provides strong evidence that the conditions of the slaves on the Ile de France were bad and, for many slaves, so intolerable that they would risk the terrible punishments which awaited them if they were recaptured after escaping. The whipping and chaining of slaves were common forms of punishment as was branding on the shoulder with a *fleur-de-lis*. A slave recaptured after a second escape would probably lose a limb by amputation.

Slaves performed many kinds of work on the Ile de France. The island's economy was still far from being dominated by the cultivation of sugar as it came to be in the next century. It was still grown for home use only as there was no outlet for it on the export market. Many slaves did, however, work in agriculture, growing sugar or one of the island's other crops at this time. Some worked in the mills where the sugar was crushed. Others worked as domestic servants, an occupation in which Indians were given preference. A special class of slaves were known as royal slaves (*esclaves du roi*) and worked for the government on the upkeep of roads and bridges.

Estate slaves were housed in small, one-roomed thatched huts in slave compounds or *camps des noirs* which were usually close to the homes of their masters. They were subjected to harsh discipline under a camp commandant whose chief instrument of punishment was a whip. Working hours were long, beginning soon after dawn and continuing until late afternoon with only one break for food around midday. Each slave was allotted a small patch of land round his hut. By cultivating this he could vary his diet and perhaps earn a little money by selling part of his own produce. In this way a few slaves were eventually able to purchase their freedom. Slaves might also be freed (*affranchis*) as a reward for long and loyal service. In either case, however, emancipation could be granted only with government permission.

There was one way in which slaves might try to relieve the monotony and harshness of their lives. Many seem to have kept alive the culture of their former homes in parts of Africa or elsewhere in song and dance. Sundays and festivals could be enlivened by dancing and music making. The origins of the *Sega*, a dance still performed on the island, are thought to go back to the days of the slave trade and to have been brought to the island by African slaves.

French headquarters in the Indian Ocean

A final mark of honour was conferred upon the Ile de France at the very end of the period of royal administration. Since 1735 it had been the seat of government for the Mascarene Islands. In 1789, during the governorship of Raymond d'Entrecasteaux, it replaced Pondicherry, by now an unfortified possession in an area dominated by the British, as the French headquarters in the Indian Ocean. In the same year the Revolution began in France. Within two years its effects were being felt in the Ile de France.

Suggestions for revision

You should know:

a) the main achievements of the French during the period of royal administration between 1767 and 1790;

b) the system of government and administration in the Ile de France and the Mascarenes under royal administration and how this compares with that under the East India Company;

c) the work and importance of the main personalities of the period, including Poivre, Suffren, Souillac and Tromelin;

d) about the growth and development of Port Louis;

e) the main facts about slaves on the island; where they came from; how many of them there were; their living and working conditions.

Suggestions for further work

1 Compare the role of Port Louis in the war of 1778 to 1783 with its role in the Seven Years' War, 1756-1763.

2 How and why did the island become more prosperous under royal rule than it had been under Company rule?

3 Find out more about the life and work of Poivre, Suffren, Souillac and Tromelin.

4 Make sure you know the meaning of the following words: segregation (page 22) and corsairs (page 23).

CHAPTER 5

The French in Mauritius
3 The Revolutionary period, 1790-1803

First reactions

The first news of the Revolution of 1789 to reach the Ile de France was brought by a ship from Bordeaux at the end of January, 1790. To understand the effect of such news on the people of the island, particularly the Europeans, it is necessary to remember the island's political and geographical position and also the political situation in France between 1790 and 1800.

The Ile de France was so lonely and so remote from France that it was difficult to verify and to understand the significance of the news brought from France by visiting ships. The news that arrived early in 1790, for example, must have indicated to all who were capable of some understanding of such events that the King's authority had been seriously challenged. Between that time and the news of the King's execution, which reached the island in April 1793, all that was clear to the people in the Ile de France was that the royal authority was declining and then that it had altogether collapsed. The political situation in France remained unsettled until the rise of Napoleon after 1799 brought the return of firm rule and more stable conditions. During these years the news arriving periodically from France must often have been conflicting and confusing. It is not surprising that these years should have been years of change and uncertainty on the island.

Administrative changes

When the first news of revolution reached the island in 1790 the settlers were generally sympathetic. The fact that Governor Conway clearly disapproved of the news merely confirmed this attitude. He was unpopular and his authoritarian style of rule was generally disliked. For many he must have embodied in his manner and his approach to government the arbitrary character of the *ancien régime*. The islanders soon wanted to follow the precedents set in France and favoured the setting up of an assembly in the colony. Conway tried to prevent them but he finally had to give way. A meeting was held at the end of April 1790 in the parish church of Port Louis and out of this meeting emerged a 'General Assembly' of the colony.

Disputes soon developed between the newly created body and the governor. One of these concerned the vital matter of the oath of allegiance taken by the members of the armed forces. The governor wanted this to be a private ceremony held in the barracks; the assembly wanted it to be held in public before the 'nation'. In the end the assembly had its way and an oath-taking ceremony was held on the Champ de Mars. Other developments followed those which were taking place in France as more news came through. A National Guard replaced the island's militia. In June 1790 a decree which had been passed by the National Assembly in Paris reached the Ile de France. The decree recommended that the islanders should elect their own legislative assembly. The General Assembly already in existence now took the name of the Colonial Assembly with the authority of the decree behind it. Local district councils were set up and became the first genuine form of local government to operate on the island. The district communes which had previously existed under the royal administration were little more than local organisations which tried to ensure that roads were kept in a reasonable state of repair. The new local councils were confirmed when the National Assembly in Paris officially recognised the new Colonial Assembly in April 1791.

Governor Conway, who had been out of sympathy with all these changes from the start, resigned his post in July 1790 and was replaced by Charpentier de Cossigny who remained governor for the next two years. They were critical years for France and for the Ile de France. He generally accepted the changes proposed by the Colonial Assembly. These included a wholesale renaming of streets and other public places. Of the old names commemorated in this way only the most famous and distinguished survived. These included Labourdonnais, Poivre and Suffren. All others were swept away in the new fashion. A new Colonial Assembly was elected and slowly, along with the district and municipal councils, began to take over the real powers of government. Cossigny and the few surviving officials under him, still nominally servants of the Crown, kept very much in the background.

A striking warning had already been given to any royalist supporters and opponents of revolutionary change. Count McNamara, the Irish-born commander of the French fleet in the Indian Ocean, had put into Port Louis in 1790. He was more loyal to the monarchy than Conway. He was suspected of organising resistance to the changes taking place in the Ile de France; he was arrested and brought before the Colonial Assembly. Early in November 1790, whilst he was being escorted to prison, he tried to escape but was brutally hacked to death by the soldiers. There were a few other outbursts of violence in 1791 and some signs that men with extreme views were gaining influence.

Revolutionary fervour was dampened down, however, by the outbreak of a serious epidemic of smallpox in June 1792. It began amongst some recently imported slaves and spread rapidly. Before the epidemic abated in October several thousand people, estimated at about 8 per cent of the population, had died.

The governorship of Malartic

A new governor, General Malartic, arrived to take over from Cossigny while the epidemic was still raging. Although the King, Louis XVI, was still alive, he was by this time powerless and Malartic was appointed by the revolutionary authorities in France. He remained governor until his death eight years later in June 1800 and served the Ile de France well in a difficult period.

At times Malartic may have been rather like the reed that bends but does not break. He certainly moved with the main tide of opinion which, on the whole, was moderate or even conservative, and he managed to curb the activities of revolutionary extremists. During what was undoubtedly the island's most critical moment during his governorship he stood by the Colonial Assembly in defying the orders of the revolutionary government in France.

This was the result of the legislation, passed first by the National Assembly and then confirmed in 1794 by the Convention, to abolish slavery. The decision had little practical impact inside France. It was a matter of life and death for French settlers and plantation owners in her colonies in the Caribbean and in the Indian Ocean. The issue came to a head in the Ile de France in 1796 but it is necessary to see it as the central point in Malartic's governorship.

He arrived in the island with a group of commissioners whose job was to see that the principles and the laws of the Revolution were carried out. Already much had been achieved to implement the work of the Revolution in the Ile de France. It had a Colonial Assembly and local councils and it had successfully crushed what little attempt there had been at counter-revolution. Quite simply the comparatively small number of Europeans and free citizens were enjoying the new experience of being able to exercise some power after the autocratic rule of royal officials.

The tomb of General Malartic, Mauritius 1840

Radicals versus moderates

As in France, however, support for the revolution took different forms. Some supporters were more extreme and more radical than others. The Ile de France produced the equivalent of the Jacobins in France. They were in fact local Jacobins. They organised themselves into clubs which were known in the Ile de France as 'chaumières' after the most famous of all their clubs, 'La Chaumière', which was founded in Port Louis in 1793. They probably played an important part in the proceedings which ended in the death of the unfortunate McNamara. They became active again after the smallpox epidemic and they were given new hope and encouragement by the news from France in 1793 and 1794. The King was executed in January 1793. The French Jacobins, partly by the use of force and well-organised coups, gained control over the Convention and were responsible for setting up the machinery of the Reign of Terror; the Revolutionary Tribunal, the Committee of General Security and, above all, the Committee of Public Safety. They governed France from April 1793 to July 1794. They saved the Revolution from the internal and external forces which threatened to overthrow it. Their most important leader was Robespierre.

The Jacobins in the Ile de France never achieved the same influence as their counterparts in France. In the island there was nothing which was remotely like the serious counter-revolutionary threats which, more than anything else, had enabled the Jacobins to gain supreme power in France. The local Jacobins arrested the senior naval officer in 1794 as a suspected enemy of the Revolution but even this seemed too extreme an action to the Colonial Assembly, whose members realised that their own interests might be threatened if the 'chaumières' became too powerful.

In France the Jacobins were so successful in crushing the internal risings and driving back the foreign armies that had invaded France that the moderate revolutionaries began to argue that the Reign of Terror was no longer justified. There was a growing movement against Robespierre and those of his colleagues who were still stepping up the Terror; and, in the famous *coup d'etat* of Thermidor (July) 1794, Robespierre became one of the last victims of the Terror, which he had done so much to create and sustain. News of the fall of Robespierre and the end of the Committee of Public Safety in Paris reached Port Louis and in November 1794 the 'chaumières' ceased to be a serious threat. There were short-lived and unsuccessful attempts by the Jacobins in the Ile de France to make a comeback in 1798 and in 1799. In 1798, for example, a small group of Jacobins actually held control of Port Louis for a few days but they were obliged to surrender to a force which marched on the capital from the countryside.

The issue of slavery

The episode which showed clearly that the majority of the supporters of the Revolution in the Ile de France were moderates occurred in 1796. A naval squadron under the command of de Sercey arrived in Port Louis from France on 18 June 1796. It brought two battalions of French soldiers and two commissioners called Baco and Burnel. They had orders to enforce the law abolishing slavery which had been confirmed in February 1794 during the Reign of Terror. Sympathetic though the members of the Colonial Assembly might have been to other revolutionary laws, they were united against this particular law. The economy of the island was built on the existence of a large slave population. Nearly 50,000 of the island's population of about 60,000 were slaves. It would have been far too dangerous to set free such a large number of slaves. The Assembly, with the Governor's support, ordered the expulsion of Baco and Burnel. The troops they had brought with them remained. There was a danger for a short time that they might rebel, but the National Guard was able to confine them to their barracks and the danger passed.

The consequences of this incident were very important both for France and for the colony. The authorities on the island had openly defied a French law and the French government's representatives sent especially to enforce its observance. Until General Decaen was received by the islanders seven years later the Ile de France was, in practice, an independent territory.

The role of the corsairs

The position of the Ile de France between 1796 and 1803 was precarious. It was a French possession which had rejected French control in the middle of a war against Britain. Its protection after 1796 depended almost entirely on the activities of its corsairs. Admittedly they were numerous and their exploits as commerce raiders reached a new peak under captains like Lemême, Hodoul, Malroux, Le Vaillant, Dutertre and Robert Surcouf, who was beginning to build up his reputation as the 'king of the corsairs'. For a short time the naval squadron of de Sercey, which had brought the two commissioners Baco and Burnel to the Ile de France, joined the corsairs in attacking British shipping. Between 1793 and 1802, 119 prizes were taken and the booty captured from them was estimated to have been worth £2½ million. So valuable were the goods captured that the island's trade actually increased, with ships from neutral countries like America and Denmark playing a large part in the commerce.

The survival of the Ile de France in these years depended on three main factors: the activities of the corsairs; the trade their prizes generated with neutral countries; and the preoccupation of Britain's navy with other more vital concerns than the Ile de France. The island was threatened only once by a British naval force in the early stage of the war. This was in 1794, when a British force approached the island but withdrew when attacked by Renaud who had just taken over the command of the French naval forces in the Indian Ocean from St Félix. From that time until the tightening of the blockade by Britain after 1806 (see Chapter 7) the corsairs were safe in their base at Port Louis and this went a long way to explain the remarkable success of their operations in the last years of the Revolutionary War (1793-1802).

Economic stagnation

Unfortunately the economic position of the Ile de France was weakened by the disastrous practice of printing too much paper money. It was a policy which had undermined the financial position of the island since the last years of Company rule and which led to violent fluctuations in the value of the island's money. During the revolutionary period the paper money became practically worthless.

It should, therefore, come as no surprise that little was achieved on the island during these years by way of improvements to the buildings and other facilities of Port Louis. It was a period of marking time in this respect. The site of the municipal market was moved in 1790 to the old Company's garden but there was no money to erect new market buildings on the site. A private individual, Thuillier, undertook to build a public hall as well as market buildings in return for the lease of part of the site. The scheme was begun but eventually abandoned for lack of funds. Another promising and much needed scheme which also had to be left unfinished was a plan to improve the water supply to the eastern end of the town. The parish church which was destroyed by a cyclone in 1773 and rebuilt after a long delay between 1778 and 1782, was again closed in 1795 because it was in a dangerous condition. The new revolutionary municipal council in Port Louis was without an adequate, permanent home because there was no money to build a town hall.

The revolutionary government could, however, claim one achievement. It was an important one because it showed the government was anxious to apply some of the ideals of the Revolution. The first school had been opened in Port Louis in 1764 and in 1778 the abbé Quinlan became head of the island's first 'college'. But there was no general system of education and in 1791 one of the early decisions of the Colonial Assembly was to make the municipal council responsible for education. At first it did little to discharge its responsibility apart from making grants from municipal funds to several private schools. In 1800, however, a new school, the Central School of the Ile de France and the Ile de Bourbon, was built on land bought by the Assembly. It was a case of better late than never. But at least a start had been made in the provision of education by the public authorities on the island.

Suggestions for revision

The main theme here is the impact of the

Revolution in France on the Ile de France.
You should know:

a) how the system of government in the Ile de France changed between 1790 and 1803;
b) about the work and importance of Governor Malartic and Robert Surcouf.

Suggestions for further work

1 Why did the people of the Ile de France initially welcome the news of the Revolution in France and later defy the revolutionary government in Paris?
Describe one incident which shows the first reaction and another which shows the second.

2 Suggest reasons why Jacobins in the Ile de France never succeeded in dominating the political life of the islands as they had done for a time in 1793 and 1794 in France.

3 Suggest reasons why the Ile de France became a particularly suitable base for the operations of pirates and corsairs between 1793 and 1807.

4 Make sure that you understand the references in this chapter to people and political institutions in France during the French Revolution: National Guard and National Assembly (page 27), Convention (page 48), Reign of Terror, Committee of Public Safety, Revolutionary Tribunal and Jacobins (page 29).

CHAPTER 6

The French in Mauritius
4 The Napoleonic period, 1803-1810

One reason the people of France and the Mascarene Islands were ready to accept the rule of Napoleon was that the revolutionary governments had failed to bring prosperity. For most of the period 1790 to 1800 prices had been rising. Nothing is more certain to make a government unpopular.

The restoration of links with France

Napoleon's rise to political power began in France with the *coup d'état* of Brumaire in 1799. The Ile de France continued to manage its own affairs independently of France for nearly four more years. Napoleon let it be known that he was prepared to allow slavery to continue in the Mascarenes. This prepared the way for the restoration of direct administrative links with France in 1803.

The restoration came about almost accidentally. Early in 1803 General Decaen was appointed by Napoleon to lead an expedition to restore French control over her posts in India and over the rebellious Mascarene Islands. Decaen was an ambitious man and regarded the restoration of French influence in India as the more important part of his task. He learned of the renewal of war the day after his arrival in Pondicherry and new instructions from France ordered him to proceed to the Ile de France.

The inhabitants of the Ile de France, already assured that slavery would be allowed to continue, welcomed him as their new governor. A decree issued in 1803 permitted the continuation of the slave trade. In one other respect the revolutionary principle of equality was ignored by the new regime. Until 1803, at least in theory, no distinction was made between different categories of free men but only between free men and slaves. Whether they were Europeans or Creoles or freed slaves, all free men had been equal before the law, though practice did not always correspond with theory. Under a decree issued in 1803 a legal distinction was made for the first time between those of pure French blood and those of mixed blood. The former were 'equal and free' the latter were only 'free'.

Administrative changes

Decaen quickly dismantled the revolutionary machinery of government without protest from the islanders. The Colonial Assembly, the district and municipal councils and the National Guard were all abolished. The government was reorganised on a system little different from that under the *ancien régime* before the Revolution. Power in the Ile de France was vested mainly in Decaen who bore the title of

Charles Mathieu Isidore Decaen

Captain-General, conferred upon him by a consular decree issued in February 1803. He was assisted by a colonial prefect and a commissioner for justice. A legion replaced the National Guard. The commander of the legion together with a police commissioner and a civil commissioner were responsible for the maintenance of law and order within the municipal boundaries of Port Louis. The boundaries of Port Louis, which had grown rapidly since its foundation by Labourdonnais, were clearly defined for the first time by one of Decaen's early decrees.

Reconstruction

Port Louis was renamed Port Napoleon shortly after Napoleon became Emperor in 1804. Decaen was concerned about the fortification of the town. It was a problem which had often been discussed since the end of the Company's rule. The defences were in an unsatisfactory state and little had been done to add to the earlier work of Labourdonnais and Cossigny because of a disagreement between two schools of thought. In the early days of royal administration the engineer Quérénet had favoured the idea of turning Port Louis into a fortified town, surrounded by an unbroken line of defences. The governor of the time, Ternay, disagreed. He felt that the scheme was wasteful and unnecessary and that there was much more essential work waiting to be carried out including the repair of cyclone damage, the rehousing of troops and civilians, road construction and the building of food stores. Others believed that the capital should rely mainly on its natural defences. In the end a start was made on Quérénet's work, but progress was slow and he left the island in 1779 with little accomplished.

Decaen reverted to Quérénet's plan to make Port Louis into a fortified town and he was able to incorporate the unfinished earlier work into his new scheme, though six years later the new defences proved to be of little use when British forces landed in the north of the island and marched on the capital (see Chapter 7).

The harbour

Decaen also recognised the need for urgent work on the harbour. Through neglect it was once again becoming silted up. The dredgers used by Tromelin thirty years earlier were again pressed into service and soon the harbour was capable of handling more and bigger ships than it had been for some time. Tromelin's plans for extending the harbour into the Caudan basin had never been put into effect; they were now developed and new shipyards were built. Decaen was also interested in the island's second harbour site on the south-east coast at Grand Port Bay. He visited the area in 1804 and founded a new town which he originally called Mahébourg and soon renamed Port Imperial. His intention was not to use Port Imperial as a port. The prevailing winds made it unsuitable for this purpose and Decaen did not intend to go back on the decision taken over seventy years earlier to site the main commercial port and naval base in the north-west at Port Louis. He believed, however, and events were soon to bear him out, that Port Imperial could have strategic importance in future wars. He fortified the Ile de La Passe which guards the entrance to Grand Port Bay. It was here, in August 1810, that the British made their initial attempt to conquer the Ile de France and suffered a serious naval defeat in the process (see Chapter 7).

Law and education

It was natural that the reconstruction in the French colonies should reflect the work carried out by Napoleon in France. This was most clearly seen in the fields of law and education. In terms of law, Decaen adapted the famous Napoleonic Codes worked out in France to the needs of the Mascarene Islands. The result, known as the Code Decaen, has remained the basis of the island's legal system. Napoleon's Civil Code, the most famous of his codes, confirmed some of the principles of the Revolution, such as freedom of worship. It also laid great emphasis on the rights of property and the protection of those rights, and thus found favour with Franco-Mauritians.

In terms of education the Central School, opened a few years earlier and already a going concern, was moved to a new site and renamed the Lycée Colonial. It was in line with similar institutions in France and was expected to turn out potential officers for the legion as well as citizens with a sound general education.

Social life
New buildings again began to be erected in the town after the stagnation and inactivity of the revolutionary period. The social life of the capital was transformed and in its spendour soon surpassed even the high standards set by Governor Souillac. In this respect Decaen had an asset in his beautiful wife who showed great talent as a hostess at the many splendid social functions which became a regular part of the life of the island. It became customary to celebrate each of Napoleon's military victories with a ball. The richer members of the community and their wives vied with one another in dress and in every aspect of fashion and display. Fine houses were well furnished and superb food was served at dinner parties and on other social occasions.

Trade and commerce
Such a flowering of the social life of the island would hardly have been possible without a revival of prosperity. The hope of such a revival was one of the main reasons for the island's ready acceptance of Decaen as their ruler when he arrived in August 1803. One of his most important and effective measures was to regulate the issue of paper money. This kept prices from rising, stabilised the currency and greatly improved the financial position of most of the 'free' islanders.

Commerce had flourished during the closing years of the *ancien régime* but had suffered a serious check at the end of the Revolutionary War. It enjoyed a vigorous revival in the short period of peace following the Peace of Amiens in 1802. With the renewal of war this was temporarily checked; but soon any setback was more than counter-balanced by the lucrative prizes taken by the island's many corsairs in their raids on British shipping. Decaen enjoyed a windfall from increased duties imposed on these captured goods. But this prosperity was quite artificial. The island was full of luxury goods from the captured British vessels; prices were high; the island was producing little of value; without food imported from Réunion it would have gone hungry.

Official French naval operations were of little significance. A small force under Admiral Linois returned to France in 1805 after its commander had fallen out with Decaen. The few naval vessels left in the Ile de France operated as commerce raiders after this date. It was not until the final years of Decaen's rule that trade began to suffer as a result of the growing effectiveness of the British naval blockade. This curbed the activities of the commerce raiders and made it more difficult for the neutral merchant ships to get through. The tightening of the blockade was made possible by Britain's recapture of the Cape in 1806, though in 1807 Surcouf, the 'king of the corsairs', had one of his most successful years. Decaen was then foolish enough to quarrel with him and seize his ship. Surcouf returned to France.

The British conquest

French hopes of military and naval success in the Indian Ocean and the East were briefly raised in 1808 when Holland was formally annexed by Napoleon and the naval and other resources of the Dutch East Indies became available to France. Unfortunately this development also had the effect of increasing Britain's resolve to conquer the Mascarene

Robert Surcouf

Islands. In 1809 the British occupied Rodrigues and in July 1810 Réunion fell with scarcely any resistance (see Chapter 7).

The fate of Réunion was not surprising because it had been badly treated during Decaen's period of rule. The loss of Réunion (the island's name had been changed from Bourbon to Réunion by the Convention in 1793) had a bad effect on the general well-being of the remaining islands, for Réunion had been the chief food producer since the beginning of the French period. Coffee was the principal crop until the coffee plantations were almost ruined by disastrous weather in 1806 and 1807. Cyclones were followed by a severe drought. The planters abandoned coffee and turned to sugar cane; but agricultural production was severely affected and famine conditions existed on the islands.

The inhabitants of Réunion had been growing accustomed, even before Decaen's time, to being treated almost as a colony of the Ile de France. The trend had begun soon after Labourdonnais had made Port Louis the headquarters for the administration of the Mascarenes. The position merely became more marked under Decaen and was at times positively discriminatory. For example Decaen transferred half of the revenue raised on exports from Réunion to the Ile de France. When, following the disastrous weather of 1806 and 1807, the planters in Réunion turned from coffee to sugar cane, Decaen protected the interests of the planters on the Ile de France by banning the production on Réunion of arrack, a distillation of the juices from sugar cane. Decaen devoted much thought and money to strengthening the defences on the Ile de France, but he quite neglected the defences of Réunion.

Once Britain had decided to capture the Mascarenes there was little that the French could have done to prevent her doing so, given the balance of naval forces in the Indian Ocean. Neglect of the defences of Réunion merely made her task easier than it might otherwise have been. In 1815 when peace was made between Britain and France, Réunion was returned to France. Britain's interests were almost purely strategic and from this point of view there had never been any doubt that the Ile de France was the more important of the two main islands. The value of the islands for agriculture and commerce, whatever the future might suggest, was of little consequence to Britain either in 1810 when she conquered them or in 1815 when their future was decided.

Suggestions for revision

You should know:

a) the main facts about the work and achievements of Decaen, Captain-General of the Ile de France, 1803-1810;
b) the story of the British conquest of the island, 1809-1810 (see also Chapter 7).

Suggestions for further work

1 Give reasons for the greater prosperity of the Ile de France under Decaen than under the revolutionary regime.
2 What enabled the British to tighten their blockade of the Ile de France in 1808 and begin their plans to conquer the island in the following year?
3 The social life of the island had one of its most splendid periods under Decaen. Try to find out more about this; about some of the great social occasions and about the fashions and homes of the leading members of the island's society.
  When had social life on the island had an earlier period of spendour?

CHAPTER 7

The Ile de France and the struggle for the Indian Ocean

As we have seen (Chapter 1), the history of Mauritius began when European merchants sailing the Indian Ocean discovered the island and began using it as a port of call. The Dutch made the first attempts at settlement, but they abandoned Mauritius in 1710, just as a new chapter in the story of the Indian Ocean was about to begin.

Changes in India

This new chapter was the result of two important changes in India. The first was the decline of the Moghul Empire, which for centuries had given India unity and order. The Emperor Aurungzeb was the last of the Moghul emperors who was able to enforce his rule throughout India and in 1707, three years before the Dutch left Mauritius, he died. Under his successors the Moghul peace crumbled. Local rulers began to exert their own authority and to make war on one another. The European merchants in India no longer felt safe. They had depended on the peace and protection of the Moghul Empire. In future they would have to protect themselves and it would be safer for them to carry on their trade in bases which belonged to their companies and which could be fortified.

The second change was that the British and French trading companies in India, the East India Company and the Compagnie des Indes, emerged as the two most powerful groups of foreign merchants. The Portuguese, the first Europeans to trade with India, had lost their important position long before 1700, although they retained their colony at Goa, which had formerly been a useful naval base. Their successors, the Dutch, were beginning to concentrate their attention on the East Indian archipelago (the present Indonesia), and were inclined to give way in India before French and British competition. The French Compagnie des Indes on the other hand was cutting down its activities in other areas and concentrating on India. By the 1730s it was represented in two of its main Indian stations by very able and ambitious men: Dumas at Pondicherry and Dupleix at Chandernagore. Dupleix could already see the opportunities presented to the French by the new conditions prevailing in India. He saw how, by making alliances with the most powerful local rulers, he might strengthen the position of the French and weaken the British.

Labourdonnais' rule

In 1735 a new governor arrived in the Ile de France (see Chapter 3). This was Mahé de Labourdonnais, an experienced sea captain in the Company's service. Like Dupleix, Labourdonnais was a man with vision and ambition, and with a good eye for the possibilities which a strong and well-developed colony in the island might bring for French interests in India. He realised that a struggle for power between France and Britain was already beginning both in the Indian Ocean and in India. He began at once the job of constructing a well-equipped and well-protected port and naval base at Port Louis: he established a shipyard and developed the small harbour settlement into a town. But in spite of Labourdonnais' great gifts of leadership, his ideas were too advanced for the Company and for the settlers. The settlers hated being made to work on his great schemes; the Company was thinking of a safe commercial harbour and did not contemplate anything so formidable as a naval base.

War of the Austrian Succession, 1740-1748

In 1740, when war broke out in Europe between Britain and France, Labourdonnais was cruising with a small fleet off the Indian coast. British merchants were alarmed by his presence; but on this occasion Labourdonnais returned to Port Louis and then, on leave, to France. He was back the next year, commissioned to take command of all French forces in the Indian Ocean, with five of the Company's ships and a landing force of 500 troops. He first went to relieve the French 'factory' or trading post at Mahé; but before he could carry out any more operations, the British and French companies in India persuaded their two governments to arrange a pact of neutrality in the Indian Ocean. The Company wanted its ships to be used for trading, not for fighting, and in 1744 it ordered Labourdonnais to send them back to France.

Having lost the Company's ships, Labourdonnais set to work to build ships in his new shipyard at Port Louis. By May 1745 he had three ships ready, and two more of the Company's ships arrived from France. The pact of neutrality soon broke down, for French and British governors in India were seeking for allies among the Indian princes and found themselves involved in the wars which the princes fought among themselves. The British sent a naval squadron to India under Admiral Peyton, which cruised along the coast and captured one French post after another.

Dupleix was now in command at Pondicherry, the headquarters of the French in India, and Labourdonnais was under his orders. He sent to Labourdonnais for help and luckily five more French ships arrived at Port Louis to strengthen the tiny squadron there. In March 1746 Labourdonnais and his fleet put to sea. He found the British fleet and defeated it; then he blockaded the British base at Madras, the headquarters of the British power in India, and forced it to surrender. The two French leaders then disagreed about the fate of Madras. Dupleix wanted to plunder the place and destroy it; Labourdonnais favoured returning it after the payment of a ransom. Since Dupleix was his superior officer, Labourdonnais was bound to carry out his orders, but he returned with his ships to the Ile de France leaving Madras undamaged. Dupleix reported the affair to France, accusing Labourdonnais of treason; Labourdonnais was recalled in disgrace, tried and convicted, and spent some years in prison. In 1748 the war was ended by the Treaty of Aix-la-Chapelle. Madras was returned to the British; the French bases that Peyton's fleet had captured were returned to France.

The fighting had created a new situation in India. The two groups of foreign merchants had fought a war on Indian territory and the Indian ruler had been unable to stop them. The open struggle between Britain and France for control of India had begun. Fighting in India continued in spite of the signing of the Treaty of Aix-la-Chapelle and, initially under Dupleix' skilful leadership, the French strengthened their position by establishing puppet rulers in the Carnatic and the Deccan. Soon, however, Clive, a clerk of the British East India Company turned soldier, was beating Dupleix at his own game and Clive's victory at the Battle of Arcot (1751) ensured that the Carnatic was under a ruler favourable to Britain. In 1754 Dupleix, who in 1746 had been responsible for Labourdonnais' downfall, was himself recalled to France in disgrace.

The Seven Years' War

Official war between Britain and France began again in 1756 and lasted until 1763. This was the Seven Years' War and proved to be the most decisive phase in the struggle between Britain and France for control of India and the Indian Ocean. Early in the war Clive secured Bengal and Bihar, the richest parts of India, for the British by his victories at Calcutta, Plassey and Chandernagore in 1757. Britain's ability to keep control of this area, however, in the long run depended on whether she could establish and retain naval control over the Bay of Bengal which commanded the approaches to the Ganges delta. The key to the Bay of Bengal was the strip of water off the coast of Coromandel near Madras; the control of this in turn depended on which side possessed the most convenient naval base for its fleets. In the coming struggle Port Louis on the Ile de France was the nearest French base to this east coast of India. It was bound, therefore, to play an important part in the war. The British and French, both now aware of the importance of India and the sea routes to India, sent fleets into the Indian Ocean. The French made an especially great effort. They sent a military

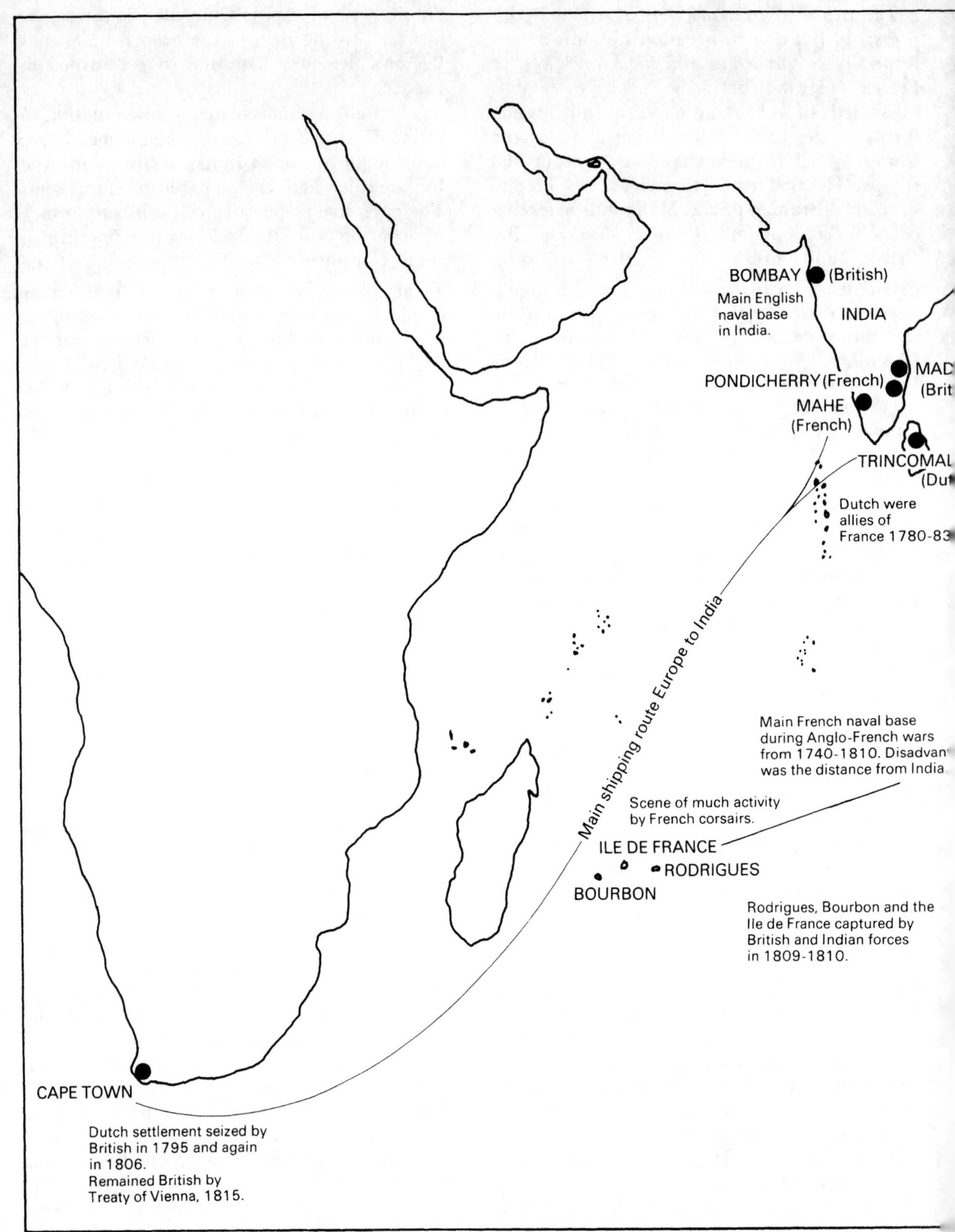

The Anglo-French struggle in the Indian Ocean 1740-1815

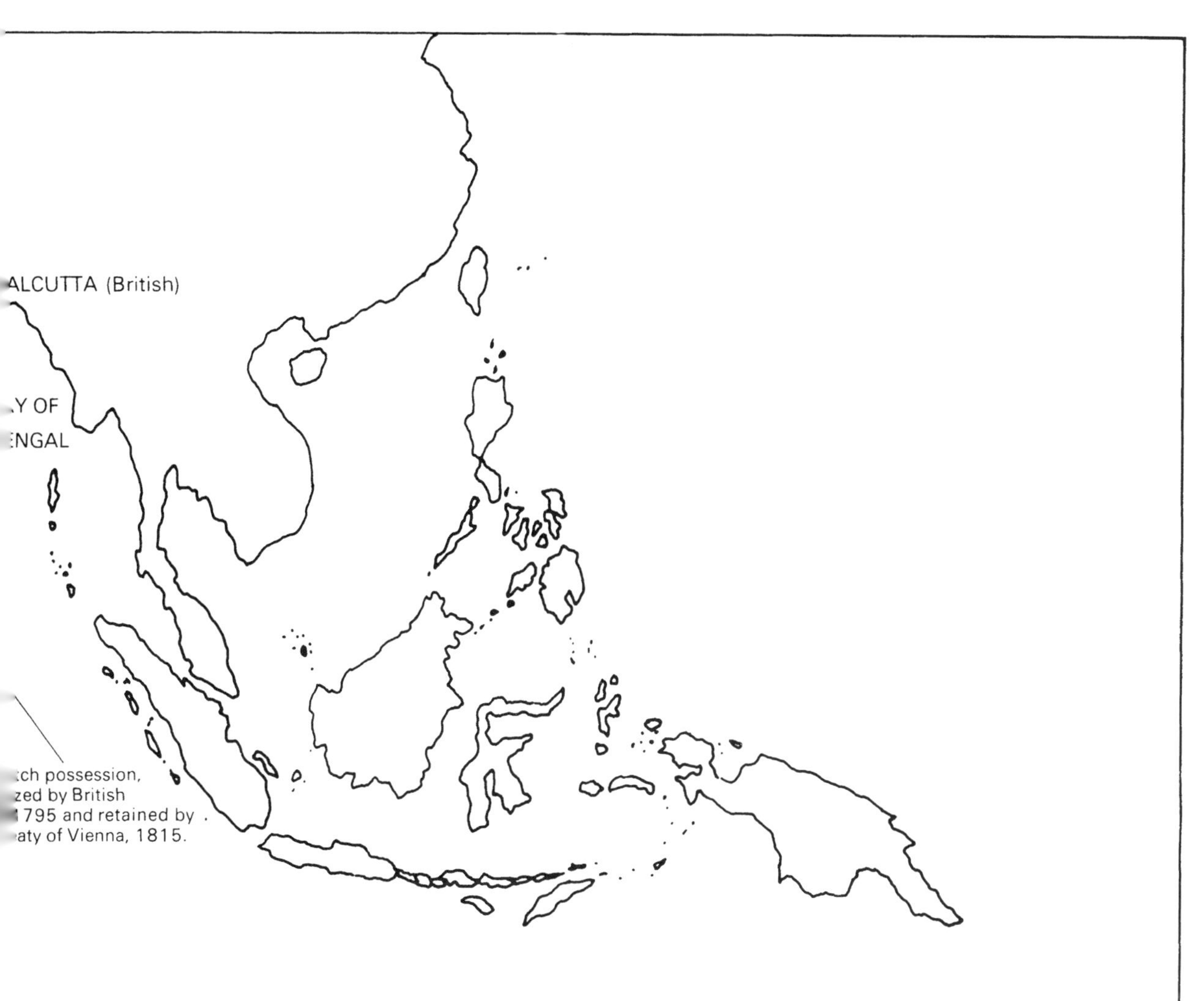

Main periods of warfare between England and France

1	1740-1748	War of Austrian Succession
2	1756-1763	Seven Years' War.
3	1778-1783	War of American Independence
4	1793-1815	Revolutionary and Napoleonic Wars

expedition under the command of Lally-Tollendal with a naval escort under Admiral d'Aché. Their aim was to drive the British from Fort St George at Madras on the Coromandel coast and, eventually, out of India altogether. After the long voyage round the Cape from France the expedition was badly in need of fresh supplies and Lally-Tollendal looked to the authorities in the Ile de France to provide them. The island, however, found difficulty in supplying the needs of such a large force; in fact with thousands of extra men to feed it was threatened with starvation. The Governor, Magon, was overwhelmed by the impossible task facing him and asked to be relieved of his post.

Lally-Tollendal put to sea and landed his troops at Pondicherry. The British admiral, Sir George Pocock, though he had failed to prevent the landing, engaged d'Aché's fleet and d'Aché withdrew to Mauritius for repairs to his damaged ships in September 1758. Magon and the settlers did what they could but it was not enough. D'Aché had to go on to the Cape for provisions and did not return to Indian waters for a whole year. Within a month he was once again forced to withdraw after an encounter with Pocock and this time he did not return. In the Ile de France he met further misfortunes: a cyclone severely damaged some of his ships as they lay in harbour and at the same time destroyed much of the island's crops. The inhabitants, desperately short of food themselves, insisted that d'Aché and his fleet should leave and d'Aché was compelled to return to France.

Lally-Tollendal and his troops in India, deprived of their naval support and with a British squadron blockading the coast, were in a hopeless position. Fort St George, previously captured by the French, was retaken by the British; Madras was saved; Pondicherry, blockaded from the sea and attacked by land, was forced to surrender. At the Peace of Paris

India 1740-1815, showing main European factories, ports and naval bases

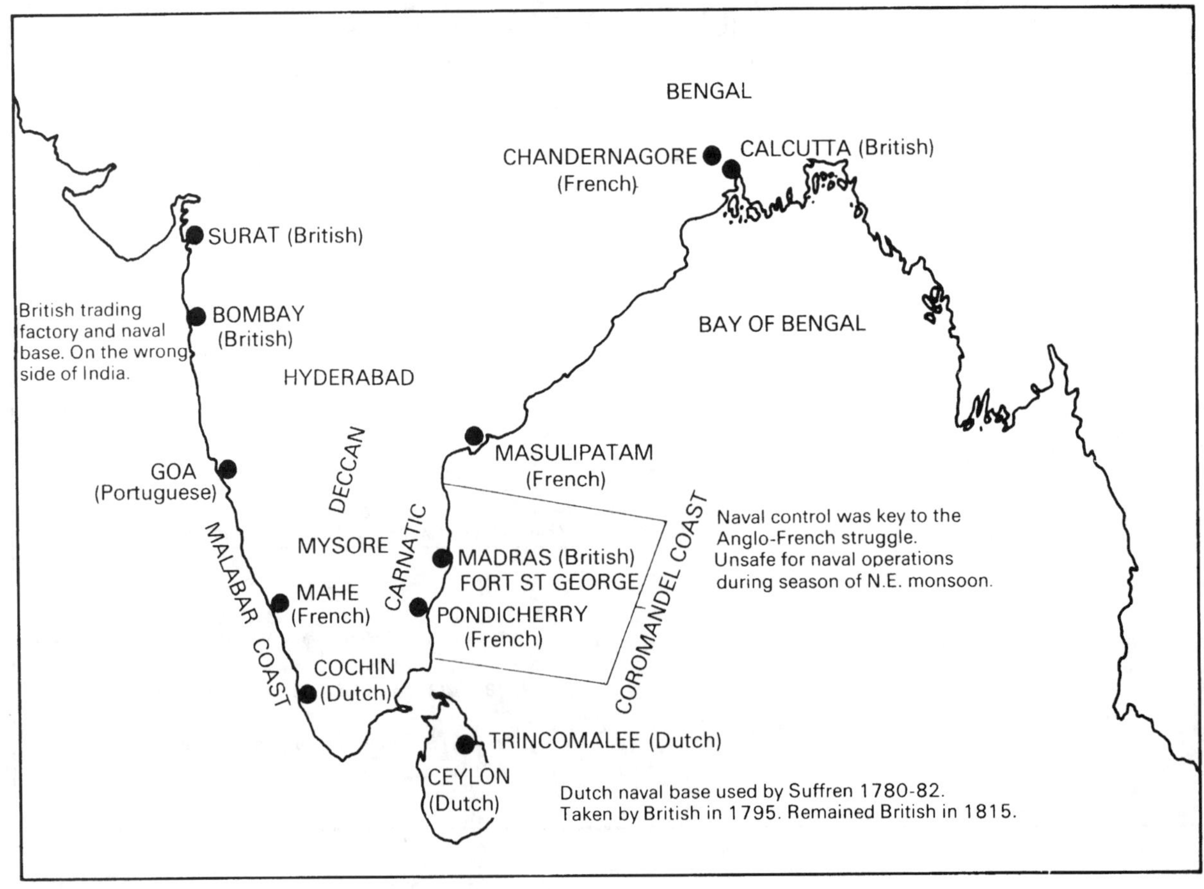

The Port Royal, *an East Indiaman*

which ended the war in 1763 the French were allowed to continue trading in India, but they were compelled to destroy all their fortifications. On his return to France the unfortunate Lally-Tollendal was executed. The French never recovered from the setbacks suffered in the Seven Years' War.

Sea power decisive

This vital campaign had been decided by sea power off the coast of Coromandel in the Bay of Bengal. The rival fleets were fairly matched, but the British base at Bombay was nearer the scene of the fighting than the French base on the Ile de France. Moreover, the voyage along the coast from Bombay to Madras was not only much shorter than the voyage from the Ile de France, it was also less stormy and dangerous for ships weakened in action. The Ile de France was not yet capable of acting as a base for such a large expedition as that of Lally-Tollendal. There were fewer than 2000 white inhabitants, most of whom hoped to make a fortune and retire with it to France, living meanwhile on the produce of their farms, which their slaves cultivated for them, and on the profits of commerce. The settlers did not see themselves either as the staff of a naval dockyard or as farmers charged with the duty of growing as much food as possible to be stored for supplying the needs of an army and its supporting fleet.

Corsairs and commerce raiding

With d'Aché and his fleet gone, the French had no hope of commanding the ocean. But there was another kind of warfare open to them, which was much more suited to the temper of men who wanted to make a quick fortune. British merchant ships were coming and going between the Cape and India and there was profit to be made by capturing them. Frenchmen from the Ile de France joyfully set sail to make war on the British by commerce raiding and they were joined by naval captains, the Comte d'Estaing and others, who were sent out from France to harry the British in this way. The Ile de France became a real 'nest of corsairs' and Britain's trade with India suffered heavy losses.

The end of Company rule

The French took the lesson of their defeat to heart. The Compagnie des Indes gave up its monopoly of the Indian Ocean trade; the Ile de France and Bourbon were taken over by the French Crown; strenuous efforts were made to develop Port Louis and the island into a naval base that could support such an expedition as that of Lally-Tollendal. The Crown took over in 1767, and between then and 1788 the white population of the Ile de France more than doubled, agriculture was extended and the harbour and dockyard were developed in a way that would have delighted Labourdonnais (see Chapter 4).

The War of American Independence, 1778-1783

In 1778 the British were heavily engaged in fighting the rebellious American colonists in the War of Independence and the French saw an opportunity of gaining revenge for their defeat in the Seven Years' War. Though Dupleix was now dead, his policies lived on and from their now unfortified bases in India his successors continued to ally themselves with Indian princes in an effort to combat the growing power of the British. In southern India, Hyder Ali, Sultan of Mysore, allied himself to the French interest.

Naval power, however, remained the key to the struggle and the French forces were at first too weak to challenge the British fleet. Even when, in 1780, Holland joined France in the

Admiral Suffren

war and thus opened up the possibility that the fine harbour of Trincomalee in Ceylon might become available as a naval base to the French, the situation did not change because Sir Edward Hughes, the British naval commander, occupied the harbour.

The naval position was suddenly changed, however, when a powerful French fleet arrived in Port Louis in October, 1781. It was commanded by a brilliant admiral, Suffren. Early in 1782 Suffren captured Trincomalee from Hughes, but although several further actions were fought between the two fleets they were not decisive. Suffren was unable to destroy the British fleet. When peace came in 1783, however, he had built up a strong position. It was perhaps fortunate for the British that the war ended when it did. But they were helped by other chance developments in 1783. French military reinforcements were delayed in the Ile de France by the outbreak of a plague epidemic. Hyder Ali, their main ally, died at an inopportune moment. The British were able to hold on to Pondicherry which they had captured earlier in the fighting, but peace restored the position to what it had been in 1763 after the Seven Years' War. Six years later the French downgraded Pondicherry from its position as their headquarters in the Indian Ocean. This role was transferred in 1789 to the Ile de France.

Revolutionary and Napoleonic Wars, 1793-1815

The struggle was renewed during the Revolutionary and Napoleonic Wars after 1793. When the French overran Holland in 1794, the British seized the Dutch possessions at the Cape and in Ceylon to prevent these vital strategic bases from falling into the hands of the French. Napoleon's expedition to Egypt in 1798 was meant to be merely the first step in a great plan leading to the French invasion of India, and no doubt the seamen of the Ile de France would have been called on to play their part in supporting Napoleon and his army there. The plan, however, was cut short by Nelson's destruction of the French fleet at the Battle of the Nile. In any case the British had learned the French plans and taken steps to protect their position in India. General Wellesley attacked and captured Seringapatam, the capital of Mysore, destroying the state's value to the French as an ally.

The climax of the struggle came between 1809 and 1810. As before, when the French fleet left Indian waters, the French naval effort was turned towards commerce raiding and a group of distinguished and very successful privateers was engaged in this kind of warfare. Robert Surcouf was the best known and he, together with Lemême, Le Vaillant, Malroux, Dutertre and others brought in plunder to an estimated value of over £2½ million between 1793 and 1802. It is not surprising that the British decided that they must destroy this threat to their commerce by capturing the Ile de France.

The need became more urgent when the Dutch island of Java was brought under French control and placed under the command of Decaen, the Captain-General of the Ile de France.

The British blockade and final conquest

Under the terms of the Peace of Amiens in 1802, the British had restored the Cape to Holland, but war broke out again in 1803 and

The battle of Ile de la Passe, 23 August 1810

in 1806 the British once more took possession of the Cape and began to blockade the French islands. In 1809 they captured Rodrigues and in July 1810 Bourbon. In the following month, a British squadron under Captain Willoughby suffered a humiliating defeat off the shores of the Ile de France. Willoughby had captured the small Ile de la Passe at the entrance to Grand Port Harbour. Sighting Captain Duperré's French squadron off Grand Port, Willoughby lured the French into the harbour by hoisting the French flag over the island. The stratagem went badly wrong; some of Willoughby's gunners were ashore when the French came in; one of his ships ran aground and he was outnumbered and outgunned.

This French victory did not delay the fall of the Ile de France for long. Decaen's position was precarious. His autocratic manner had antagonised many of the inhabitants and their loyalty to the French revolutionary governments was doubtful. The British blockade was becoming tighter and Decaen had no hope of help from outside. He had only 4000 troops and in November 1810 a British force of 10,000 men landed on the north coast of the island. Most of the units in this force came from the Indian Army and were Indian troops under British officers. The troops had been assembled on Rodrigues and their landing on Mauritius was covered by a naval escort. The French made a token stand at Long Mountain but were easily swept aside by the British[1]. Decaen might have made a final stand at the fortifications outside Port Louis, but he decided that it would be foolish to waste lives in a siege which could only delay the surrender of the capital.

On 3 December 1810 Decaen capitulated on honourable and generous terms. His troops would not be treated as prisoners of war. The property, laws, customs and religion of the settlers would all be respected. Any settler who wished to leave the island would be free to do so at any time within the next two years, taking his property with him. Although the British still had much fighting to do in India, this conquest marked the end of the struggle for supremacy in the Indian Ocean. Fifty years earlier, the British statesman Pitt had said that 'As long as the French hold the Ile de France, the British will never be masters of India.' When peace was signed in 1815, the British retained the Cape, Ceylon and the Ile de France, now to be known once more by its old name, Mauritius. Together, these three possessions, if securely held, guaranteed the sea route to India for British trade.

Suggestions for revision

The story of the struggle between Britain and France for control of India and the Indian Ocean is a part of world history in which the Ile

1 *For a fuller account of this campaign see Hazareesingh, K.* History of Indians in Mauritius, *pp. 4-8. Macmillan Education Ltd. 1975*

de France played a significant role.

You should know:

a) the story of this struggle, as a whole;
b) the details of the main stages of the fighting in the war, such as 1740-1748, 1756-1763 and 1778-1783, as well as the details of the British conquest of the islands between 1809 and 1810;
c) the part played in the struggle by leading figures such as Labourdonnais, d'Aché, Lally-Tollendal, Suffren and Surcouf.

Suggestions for further work

1 Study the map of the Indian Ocean. How far was a) Bombay and b) Port Louis from the coast of Coromandel where most of the fighting took place between the rival fleets? What effect did this have on the chances of the two fleets?

2 How did the monsoons affect the naval fighting in the Bay of Bengal? When was it unsafe for a fleet to be at sea in the Bay of Bengal?

3 Make a chart of the four main wars between Britain and France during the period 1740 to 1815 and mark on it the main events in the struggle for India and the Indian Ocean.

4 Find out more about the corsairs and their activities.

5 Find out more details about the fighting in the campaigns of 1809 to 1810. In particular, learn more about the naval engagement in Grand Port Bay, the British landing in the north-west of the island and the march on Port Louis leading to the surrender by Decaen.

Imagine that you were a) a sailor in the French or British fleet in the first action and b) a soldier with the French or British forces in the second. Write your own accounts, as an eyewitness, of the fighting.

CHAPTER 8

The impact of British rule and the abolition of slavery

The British conquest of Mauritius in 1810 made little difference to the life of the island and its people. This was because of the generous capitulation terms offered to the French and summarised at the end of the previous chapter. The French were guaranteed in the possession of their property and their way of life: their language, laws, religion and customs were not to be changed. French cultural influence continued to be stronger than British. This has remained the position until very recently, when the adoption of English as the main language of education has begun to threaten the dominance of French cultural influence.

There was another reason why the British rule made comparatively little difference to life on the island. The British wanted to take control of Mauritius because whilst it remained in French hands it was a threat to the security of Britain's hold over India and to her all-important trade with India. The island of Bourbon, which had also been captured in 1810, was restored to France simply because it possessed no good harbour and therefore was considered to be of little strategic importance. The British had no plans for sending large numbers of settlers to Mauritius. They had no great expectation of carrying on a lucrative trade with the island. Their reason for taking it was essentially a negative one; to put an end to the French using it to harm British interests. So long as political and, therefore, military control remained in their hands, they were, on the whole, content to allow the French to remain in a dominant and privileged position. The French continued to dominate the economic life of the island. Most of the cultivated land was owned by French settlers and worked by slave labour.

The issue of slavery

The first serious threat that British rule posed to French interests arose when in 1807 the British Parliament passed an Act for the Abolition of the Slave Trade. This applied throughout the British Empire. In theory, therefore, it should have led to the end of the slave trade in Mauritius in 1810. In practice this did not happen. It was estimated that well over 20,000 slaves were brought into the island after it became a British possession. The first British governor, Sir Robert Farquhar, was very anxious to ensure that the period of transition to British rule should take place as smoothly as possible. He turned a blind eye to the law forbidding the trade in slaves. In 1826 the three members of a royal commission arrived in Mauritius. It was called the Commission of Eastern Enquiry and had been set up by the Colonial Office in 1822 to make recommendations concerning the future development of three of Britain's recently acquired territories: the Cape, Mauritius and Ceylon. So far as Mauritius was concerned, the Commission recommended that the island and its

Robert Farquhar

inhabitants should be 'anglicised': that English culture and the English language should come to dominate its way of life. This recommendation came to nothing and, as already noted, the island retained its essential French character. The commissioners also expressed concern about the continuation of the slave trade.

By this time, the movement in Britain against the evils of slavery was in its final stage of attacking and stamping out the institution of slavery, and not merely the trade in slaves. The Anti-Slavery Society was campaigning for the abolition of slavery without the payment of compensation to the slave owners. The members of the Society felt that, in Mauritius in particular, where the law against the slave trade had been widely ignored, there was a strong case against the payment of compensation. To pay compensation would be rewarding law-breakers. Moreover, Mauritius was a new colony, recently conquered from a foreign enemy, where the slave owners were French, not British, planters. There could be no more suitable colony for testing the principle of emancipation without compensation.

A slave presents his master with 'the rights of man'

The French case

The argument of the slave owners, whether in Mauritius or elsewhere, was that slaves were a valuable form of property and that to abolish slavery without paying compensation would be a form of robbery.

In 1830, the French planters sent one of their leaders, Adrien d'Epinay, to London to put their case for payment of compensation to the Colonial Secretary. D'Epinay received an assurance that compensation would be paid when slavery was abolished. The planters were, therefore, angry when they learned that a prominent member of the Anti-Slavery movement, John Jeremie, had been appointed as Procureur Général of Mauritius in 1832. The French planters feared that he had been sent to reopen the whole question. The Colonial Committee, a self-appointed body representing the interests of the French planters, tried to prevent Jeremie from landing and taking up his post.

General strike

The island's normal life was virtually halted by a general strike organised by the Colonial Committee. The planters appealed to the governor, Sir Charles Colville, who consulted the recently established Council of Government. The Council decided that Jeremie should be expelled in spite of his protests that he was not intending to stop the payment of compensation. The French planters seemed to have successfully defied the colonial government, but the affair was not closed. The British recalled Colville, who had agreed to expel Jeremie, and sent out Sir William Nicolay to replace him. Nicolay was accompanied by 500 soldiers. He acted swiftly to punish those who had worked for the expulsion of Jeremie. All firearms were to be surrendered; a fort was built in the centre of Port Louis. D'Epinay and the other members of the Council of Government who had supported the expulsion of Jeremie were dismissed. D'Epinay went to London for a second time to put the case of the

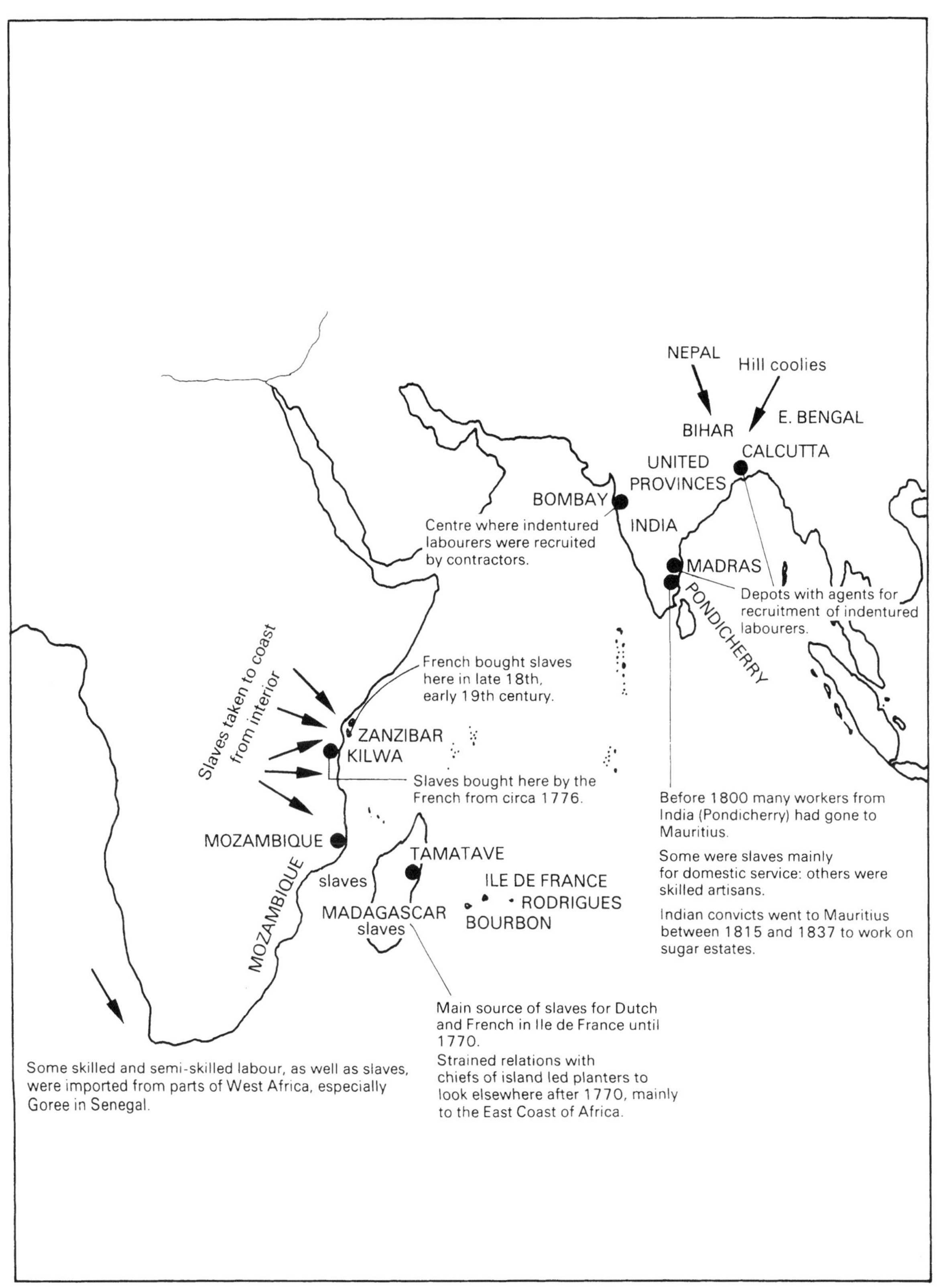

Sources of labour for Mauritius from the seventeenth to the twentieth century

planters. Jeremie returned to Mauritius while d'Epinay was in London in April 1833. He arrived with an armed escort and joined in the policy of punishing those who had been responsible for his expulsion in the previous year. Five of his opponents were arrested, charged with treason and brought to trial at Mahébourg. He went too far, however, when he tried to appoint three of his own supporters as Supreme Court judges in place of the sitting judges. The governor refused to support him in face of the outcry which arose over this move. In 1834 Jeremie was dismissed by the Colonial Secretary and recalled.

The French planters had won their struggle with the Procureur Général, whom they had distrusted and feared from the time of his appointment. It was a significant episode because it revealed clearly for the first time that British colonial officials could not easily enforce policies of which the wealthy Franco-Mauritians disapproved. There were to be other occasions during the period of British colonial rule which confirmed this important fact.

Compensation

Whilst Jeremie was being resisted successfully in Mauritius, d'Epinay, the champion and spokesman of the Franco-Mauritians, was ensuring in London that the Mauritian slave owners would receive compensation for the loss of their slaves. There were those, like the contemporary historian Albert Pitot, who believed that if d'Epinay had not been in London in 1833 and 1834 the abolitionists' attempt to prevent the Mauritian planters getting any share of the compensation money would have succeeded. The Act for the Abolition of Slavery which was passed by the British Parliament in 1833 set aside £20 million to be paid out in compensation to the slave owners and the Mauritian planters obtained just over £2 million of this sum. Considering the number of slaves in the British Empire as a whole and the number in Mauritius, this was a generous share. Although they placed a value of £4 million on their slaves the Mauritian planters knew that they had done well. On the whole they used the money wisely for the improvement and expansion of the sugar industry.

Abolition

In Mauritius the Act came into effect at the beginning of February 1835, over a year later than in most other parts of the British Empire, and could have proved disastrous to the planters and the now expanding sugar industry. Already, however, forewarned by the campaign of the abolitionists, the planters had been looking for alternative sources of cheap labour, notably in the form of immigrants from India. This soon provided the answer to the planters' urgent need for labour. In addition, the Act laid down the condition that for four years the emancipated slaves should continue to work as paid labourers on the estates of their former owners. This gave the planters a useful transitional period during which they could find alternative workers.

Emancipation

In 1839, at the end of the four years, the ex-slaves, almost to a man, left the sugar estates. To most of them, work on the sugar estates was the symbol of their earlier servitude. They preferred to take the chance, with all the insecurity it entailed, of finding other kinds of work. The theory behind the transitional period of four years was not merely that it should help the planters to weather a difficult period during which they might be short of labour; but that it should give the ex-slaves an opportunity to learn another trade if this was their wish. In practice neither the government nor the masters made any attempt to help the slaves to do this. Most of them went either into the towns or made new settlements on land so poor that nobody had so far claimed or cultivated it. There was also a lot of social prejudice against the emancipated slaves and the emerging 'coloured' populations of mixed origin. It was to fight against this social prejudice that a movement led by Remy Ollier, born in 1816, was formed to demand a more liberal treatment for them. Remy Ollier founded a paper called *La Sentinelle*, which helped him effectively in his campaign in defence of their rights. He obtained considerable fame and distinction, even in his lifetime. At this crisis period in their lives the emancipated slaves received little help or encouragement from any other whites with the exception of that from two mission priests:

Father Jean Lebrun and Father Laval. Most of them became smallholders, unskilled labourers or fishermen. A chapter in the life of the island thus ended in 1839. A new one had already begun and was soon to transform the balance of the island's population.

Suggestions for revision

Slavery and its abolition is another major topic in the history of Mauritius.

You should know:

a) how and why slave labour became established in Mauritius and where the slaves were obtained from (see also Chapter 4);
b) when and on what terms slavery was abolished in Mauritius (n.b. It is important to distinguish between the abolition of the slave trade and the abolition of the institution of slavery);
c) how the abolition of slavery affected i) the economy of the island, in both the short and long term, and ii) both the ex-slaves and the planters;
d) about the work and importance of individuals connected with the issue of slavery and its abolition on the island, such as Governors Farquhar and Nicolay, Adrien d'Epinay and John Jeremie.

Suggestions for further work

1 Find out more about the campaign for the abolition of the slave trade and of slavery itself. Would the efforts of men like Granville Sharp, Thomas Clarkso and William Wilberforce have been successful without support from other quarters? From what 'other quarters' did effective support for the abolition of the slave trade and slavery come?
2 Where else in the British Empire were slaves used as the main source of labour? What kind of work did the slaves perform in the other territories?
3 Imagine you were a slave on a Mauritian sugar plantation in the early 1830s. Describe a) your reactions on learning that you were to be freed and b) what you did after emancipation.

CHAPTER 9

The growth of the sugar industry

Expansion

If the abolition of the slave trade and of slavery itself were two of the earliest results of the establishment of British rule in Mauritius, a third effect was the rapid development and expansion of the cultivation of sugar cane. As we have seen, the growing of sugar cane was introduced into Mauritius by the Dutch. Under French rule it expanded slowly, mainly through the demand for arrack, a liquor distilled from the juices of crushed sugar cane, from French soldiers and sailors who visited the island during the Anglo-French war in the late eighteenth century.

The main stimulus to the dramatic expansion of the sugar industry came in 1825 when the British government allowed the import of Mauritian sugar into Britain on the same terms as West Indian sugar. The ending of the Anglo-French wars in 1815 was followed by a decline in Port Louis' importance as a trading port. This came about partly because Cape Town, now a British possession, was a successful rival; partly because Port Louis was no longer a free port, open to the shipping of all nations, but was hampered by the application of the Navigation Laws, which restricted the exercise of trading rights in British ports to British or locally owned ships. Governor Farquhar attempted to restore Port Louis as an open port after the disastrous fire which destroyed a large part of the town in 1816. In spite of the special circumstances, the British government at first did not approve. However, they eventually agreed to allow limited freedom of trade. The results were disappointing and the economy of Mauritius was badly in need of encouragement. The planters and the British sugar merchants tried to persuade the British government to reduce the duty on Mauritian sugar imports to Britain. The West Indian planters and merchants were, for obvious reasons, opposed to any such move. However, in 1825 the British government compromised. They agreed to allow the import of sugar from Mauritius at the same rate of duty as that from the West Indies: 12/- per cwt. Previously Mauritian sugar had been subjected to a duty of 41/- per cwt. At the same time they subjected Mauritius to a more strict operation of the Navigation Laws.

Economic importance

It is not too much of an exaggeration to claim that this decision in 1825 decided the future pattern of the Mauritian economy. The tendency over the previous half century or more for agriculture to be neglected and greater interest to be shown in commerce was reversed. Within two or three years, sugar had become overwhelmingly the most important crop grown on the island. Its production in 1826 (21,244 tons) was nearly double that in 1825 (10,869 tons). In 1840 Mauritius exported about 30,000 tons and had become the chief producer in the British Empire. By the mid-1850s it exported well over 100,000 tons. The growing of other crops, like coffee, indigo and cotton, was largely abandoned. Within six years the acreage growing sugar was doubled. The demand for sugar in Britain and other European countries was growing rapidly, though by the middle of the nineteenth century the main market for Mauritian sugar was India not Britain. The sugar industry continued to expand until the 1860s when it reached its peak for the nineteenth century. The increase in exports of Mauritian sugar from 1823 to 1860 is shown in the following table:

YEAR	1823	1827	1842	1850	1860
TONS	11,000	18,000	31,000	51,000	121,000

The Mauritian crop in 1865 was 165,000 tons.

Preparing a sugar cane field

There was then a levelling off in production and in exports followed by a slow decline, due largely to increased competition from sugar beet grown in Europe and from cheaper sugar grown in Java and Cuba. The 1865 production figure was not to be surpassed until after 1900.

Labour

The labour force had changed in two ways. With the abolition of slavery in Mauritius after February 1835, black slave labour was quickly replaced by indentured labour brought in from India. This new Indian labour force will be discussed in detail in the next chapter. The second change lay in the size of the labour force. In 1834, the last year before abolition, about 34,000 slaves were employed in the sugar fields. By 1838 the number of Indian labourers had reached 24,000. In 1846 it had risen to 50,000 and by 1870 to 216,000.

Cultivation and processing

Methods of cultivating and processing the crop were slow to change. Throughout the period, and indeed down to the present time, the cultivation of sugar in Mauritius required a very large number of labourers. Almost every part of the process, from planting to harvesting, was done manually. Much of the labour was heavy, monotonous, grinding work, especially at harvest time. Demand for labour varied according to the season. At harvest time it was at its peak and work went on day and night. The cane, once cut, had to be transported to the mill for grinding with the minimum of delay. Delay meant a fall in the quality of the sugar. Workers were driven hard by the overseers and slacking was severely punished. The following is a description of sugar production in 1858, from the planting of the cane to the bagging of the sugar. It was written in the early 1860s at a time when the industry was rapidly approaching its nineteenth-century boom years.

The land is then cleared of weeds, and holes in rows are made, about two feet apart, in which the cane is planted: these are from twenty to twenty-four inches in length, and several inches broad and deep, and at the bottom of them a little manure is put, if required. The top of the cane is cut off, and serves as food for cattle and for planting ... In December, January and February, which are considered as *grande saison*, the shootings generally appear above ground in fifteen or twenty days and when about one foot high they are weeded, and frequently a portion of the earth is taken out of the holes to liberate the young plant ... The process of weeding is continued from time to time until the cane is ripe ... The cane is then from six to nine feet in height, and is ready to be cut. The planting, weeding and cutting are done by gangs of Indians under the charge of Overseers. For the cutting, every man is furnished with a serpe (a kind of billhook) with one stroke of which he separates the cane at the bottom and with another the tender part at the top. He then strips off the withered coverings with which the cane is partly enveloped, and lays the latter aside ready for the mill . . . After the first crop, the cane without being replanted annually, springs up for a period extending from three to nine years . . . The land is then either abandoned for a time or planted with ambrevades, peas, or other vegetables and left so generally for three years . . .

In Mauritius . . . at the present day the wind and water mills of olden times have nearly all been supplanted by steam. The canes on being cut are carted to the mill . . . Leading from the door to the cylinders is an inclined wooden plane on which canes are pushed forward and are drawn in and crushed between the cylinders. They are then passed underneath . . . and spread out to dry. *Bagasse* . . . being used as fuel, it assists in feeding the furnace . . . As the juice is expressed between the cylinders it passes through a strainer and flows into the first boiler of the battery . . . It is in this state called *Flangourin* or *Vesou*. The battery is in a range of boilers or pans, four or five in number, having a furnace burning underneath, the heat of which gradually increases from the first to the last pan in which the sugar is being cooked . . . It is then passed . . . to a large flat wooden case . . . where it remains till it is cool . . . When cool . . . the molasses or syrup drops . . . This syrup is either put back in the pans to be reboiled or it is sent to the still . . . and is converted into rum. The sugar after remaining in the boxes for about a fortnight is taken out and spread in the sun to dry. It is then put into double bags . . .[1]

The process for extraction of the juices and the manufacture of sugar described here is the one known as the 'common process'.

By the time this was written steam had replaced wind and water to drive machinery in the mills. Little else had changed, however, in the manufacturing process. It was not until the 1860s or later that further change came with advances in technology. The most important of these was the introduction of the vacuum pan process. This was first developed in the USA in the 1840s. It gradually replaced the 'common process' in Mauritius and in other British sugar colonies. The advantages of the new process were greater efficiency in extraction of the juices, an increased yield from the cane and a more reliable quality of finished sugar. The disadvantage was the heavy capital cost of the machinery.

Effects on estate organisation: numbers of factories; size of estates

The new process inevitably brought important changes in organisation. It was no longer possible for each estate to have its mill for processing its own cane. In 1853 Mauritius had 222 sugar factories, in 1892 there were 104 and in 1908 the number had fallen to only 66.

Strangely enough, during the period when the number of factories was falling, the number of estates was increasing and their size was diminishing. The trend had been for estates to get fewer and larger. Many of them were financed and run by English capitalists taking advantage of expanding markets which were created partly by falling prices which more consumers could pay. Sugar consumption in Europe grew enormously during the nineteenth century. In 1820 the average consumption of sugar per person in Britain was 16.8 pounds (7.6 kg). In 1860 the consumption had risen to 34.8 pounds (15.8 kg). This had benefited Mauritius and other growers and helps to explain the great expansion of sugar cultivation throughout those years.

By 1880 British consumption had almost doubled again and was 61.8 pounds (28.1 kg) per head. But Mauritius no longer benefited from this rise in consumption. Other growers like the Cubans and Javanese were producing sugar more cheaply from cane. There was no longer any duty to pay on sugar imported to Britain which was by this time a free-trade country. At the same time European farmers were growing less corn and more sugar beet, sometimes with the help of government subsidies. From the early 1860s to the mid 1880s sugar prices had remained fairly steady.

1 *From John Anderson,* A Descriptive Account of Mauritius, its Scenery, Statistics etc., *Mauritius, 1858, p. 69. Quoted in Hugh Tinker,* A New System of Slavery, *OUP, 1974*

Between 1883 and 1887 the wholesale price in London fell from 20/11d per cwt[2] to 12/1½d per cwt. The sugar boom for Mauritius was over for the time being.

One result of this was that the planters began to sell off parts of their large estates, sometimes in small lots which were called 'morcellements'. The buyers were usually Indians who had managed to save enough to buy a smallholding. Many of these peasant cultivators were the sirdars or overseers, the elite amongst the indentured immigrants. By the beginning of the twentieth century peasant style agriculture formed a significant part of the sugar production and over 30 per cent of the cultivated land was owned by Indians. The process continued until about 1920.

This was a healthy development in the sense that it allowed some Indians to become landowners and producers instead of merely labourers. However, there were disadvantages also. Most of the land which the estate owners sold off in this way was the poorer land. Only heavy investment, which the new owners could not afford, could have made such land really productive. Most of the Indians also failed to use the best and most efficient methods of cultivation.

The introduction of improved practices had been largely the work of the big planters in the middle years of the century when estates were being consolidated. In 1840 there were 4000 planters, by 1870 there were only 1600. Fertilisers were increasingly used; irrigation canals were introduced to raise crop production; new machinery was installed in the factories. In 1853 the Chamber of Agriculture was set up. One of its aims was to encourage planters to exchange ideas and knowledge with a view to improving methods of cultivation and raising production.

Communications improvements

Improvements in communications were a feature of the nineteenth century. These were partly stimulated by the needs of the sugar industry and in turn they helped to boost the industry in various ways. The coming of the railways in the 1850s and 1860s coincided with the most rapid period of expansion for the sugar industry. To a large extent they were constructed to meet the need of the industry for quicker and easier transportation of the processed sugar from the factories to Port Louis for export. It was the Chamber of Agriculture which put forward plans for the construction of the first railways in Mauritius in 1857. These were for the Northern and Midland lines. Construction started in February 1862. The Northern line ran from Port Louis to Grande Rivière S.E. via Flacq and Pamplemousses and was finished in May 1864. The Midland line, from Port Louis to Mahébourg via Plaines Wilhems, opened in October 1865. The construction of these two lines in little over three years was a great achievement. One historian has called it 'the most successful enterprise ever undertaken in the history of the island until the cyclone reconstruction programme of the 1960s'.

Eventually the network of railways was extended. In 1878 Souillac was linked to Rose Belle on the Midland line. Two years later Flacq, already served by the Northern line, was linked with Rose Hill on the Midland line via Moka. Finally, in 1904 Richelieu was joined with Tamarin.

Sugar could now be transported easily and cheaply to Port Louis from which regular shipping services by British companies began to operate to Europe from 1852. Before 1860 there were links with India, Australia and Suez. The most permanent of the shipping services, however, was that begun in 1864 by a French company, the Messageries Impériales (later the Messageries Maritimes). The opening of the Suez Canal in 1869 greatly shortened the time and direct sailing distance to Europe but, as will be seen later, the Suez Canal brought disadvantages as well as advantages to Mauritius (see Chapter 11, page 69).

One thing was certain: the first fifty years of British rule saw the establishment of sugar growing as the dominant factor not only in the Mauritian economy, but also in the life and well-being of most of its people. Amongst other things it brought in its train the urgent need to develop the island's communications. It also

2 *1 cwt (hundredweight) = 50.8 kg. The money value is that operating at the time.*

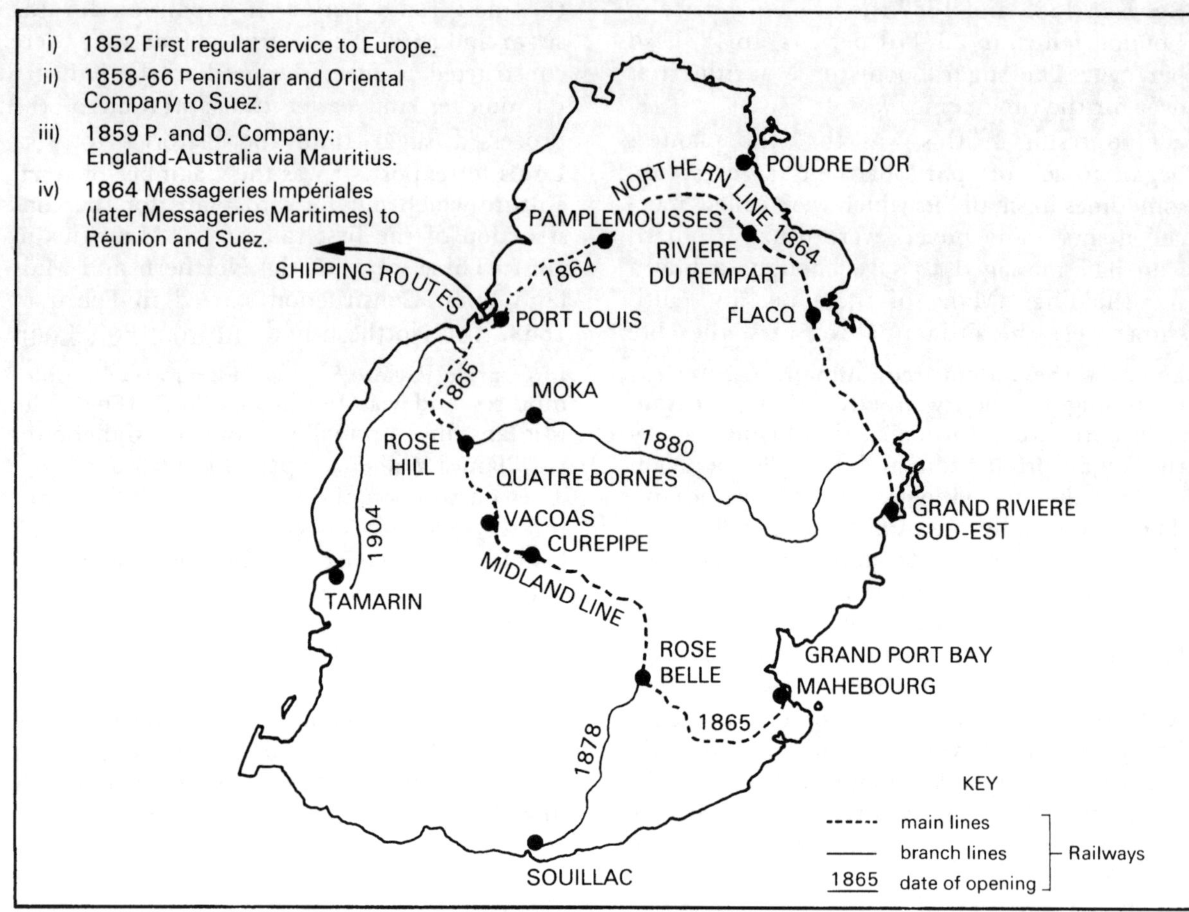

Mauritius: communications, railways and shipping lines, in the nineteenth and twentieth centuries

led to the other outstanding important development of the nineteenth century: the immigration of some 400,000 Indians. They not only provided the labour force for the expanding sugar industry, they also completely changed the balance and composition of the island's population.

Suggestions for revision

The story of the growth of the sugar industry is another key topic.
You should know:

a) why the industry expanded rapidly from *circa* 1820 to *circa* 1865;
b) why production and exports levelled off after that date until more recent times;
c) what changes took place in
   i) the nature and size of the labour force,
   ii) methods of cultivation,
   iii) methods of processing the crop,
   iv) the ownership and size of estates;
d) what the main changes in communications (railways and shipping) were and how these changes affected the growth of the sugar industry.

Suggestions for further work

1 What is meant by the sentence, 'Sugar growing in Mauritius was a labour intensive branch of agriculture'? The opposite of 'labour intensive' is 'capital intensive'. What does this mean? Why is it unlikely that the sugar industry in Mauritius will ever become capital intensive?

2 Draw a map of Mauritius and mark on it the railway lines constructed in the nineteenth century with dates showing when each line opened. Mark also the main concentration of sugar estates and sugar growing.

CHAPTER 10

Indian immigration and the growth of the Indian community in Mauritius

Transportation of slaves and convicts

There were Indians in Mauritius long before the immigration of indentured labourers began in the 1830s. Labourdonnais had encouraged Indians with skills and trades to come to the island when he was laying the foundations for its future between 1735 and 1746. In the second half of the eighteenth century Indians were to be found amongst the slaves working in agriculture and as domestic servants. Most of them came from southern India, from the region now within Kerala state. By 1800 there were around 6000 Indian slaves in Mauritius. At the beginning of the British period in 1815 groups of Indian convicts were brought to Mauritius. At the time Indian convicts were to be found in other places in south-east Asia, including Penang and Singapore. It was Governor Farquhar who asked that some of them should be sent to Mauritius, where labour was required for road building.

Charles Darwin, the famous British naturalist and scientist, called at Mauritius in April and May 1836 on the later stages of his voyage round the world in HMS *Beagle*. He commented in his diary on the Indian convicts on the island, of whom he said there were about 8000. He was impressed by their noble appearance. 'These convicts are generally quiet and well conducted; from their outward conduct, their cleanliness and faithful observance of their strange religious enactments, it was impossible to look at these men with the same eyes as our wretched convicts [i.e. convicts from Britain] in New South Wales.'

The beginning of indentured labour

In 1837, the year after Darwin's visit, the transportation of Indian convicts to Mauritius was ended. Already, however, the first trickle of indentured Indian labourers had reached the island. It had become clear in the early 1820s that the days of slave labour in the British Empire were soon to end. In 1829 representatives of the planters had made enquiries from the governments of Madras and Singapore about obtaining Indian labourers on contract. Small numbers arrived in Mauritius in 1830 and 1834. In 1835 immigration began on a regular basis. This no doubt is why the Mauritian planters were apparently so little concerned about the emancipation of their slaves during Darwin's visit. He reported: 'I was, however, surprised to find how little the few people with whom I conversed seemed to care about the subject [i.e. the emancipation of slaves]. Feeling confident in a resource in the countless population of India, the result of emancipation was here much less regarded than in the West Indies.' This was perhaps surprising in view of the Hindus' well-known objections, on religious grounds, to crossing the sea. Events soon proved that the Mauritian planters' lack of concern was justified. For the next seventy years the trickle of immigrants became a steady flow, and occasionally a flood, as the planters persistently strove to ensure that the supply of indentured labourers was always large enough to keep the cost of labour low.

Causes

The social and economic condition of India under British colonial rule enabled the recruitment of labour despite the traditional caste prejudices against crossing the seas. As the historian N. Gangulee has pointed out it was the disintegration of Indian rural life brought about by the new property laws introduced by the British that created a massive supply of unskilled labour.

For instance, in the Manbhum and Dhalbhum districts of the Chota Nagpur in South Bihar, there was widespread anger at the British administrative system, and with its alien officials infringing on local customs. This led to the Bhumij Rebellion of 1832-33 which was brutally suppressed, with great loss of life and property. This caused the displaced agricultural labourers to seek to emigrate to places where they could make a living without harassment. Many of these labourers from Chota Nagpur were well suited for work on the sugar cane plantations as they had plenty of experience of working in the hills and jungles.

Moreover, in the Bengal Presidency in the first half of the nineteenth century, the importation of foreign cotton led to the destruction of the old handicraft industry. As a result, a large number of weavers, spinners, dyers, bleachers, and needleworkers lost their occupations. In addition, the establishment of new land relations based on private property, with contract replacing custom led to a large number of the agricultural population losing their land rights. The consequent poverty made them particularly receptive to ideas of migration.

The densely populated Tamil districts of Madras with their large numbers of landless labourers were also extremely vulnerable to emigration. A recruiter called Tyack visited the Western Malabar Coast from Anjna to Cuddalore in 1838 and enlisted a large number of labourers after paying them three months wages in advance. The contract for plantation labour was for five years with the wages fixed at five rupees per month besides free food and clothing.

During the years 1858-59, emigration from India reached a peak. The great Rebellion of 1857-58 created havoc throughout northern India, from Delhi to Patna. Many lost their homes, land and livelihood, and were willing to accept the opportunity of a new life beyond the seas. Some had been directly involved in the revolt, as sepoys or other fighters, and emigration was certainly preferable to arrest, imprisonment and confinement in Port Blair.

Besides these 'push' factors in India, the almost insatiable demand of the Mauritian planters also constituted a 'pull' factor of the utmost importance. In 1855 the planters were allowed to introduce labourers at their own expense and to use the machinery of both the official Calcutta agency and the immigration office in Port-Louis. When even this system failed to produce the desired result, the planters began sending some of their own experienced labourers who were given the task of enticing as many workers as possible to embark for Mauritius. This introduced a class of middlemen, who made huge profits, into the system.

The new system

There is no doubt that the efforts of the planters to achieve their objective were successful. They created a situation in which all the benefits and advantages were on their side. They succeeded in dominating the economy and they were able to prevent the authorities from interfering effectively, in the interests of the immigrants, in the operation of the indenture system. The Indian labourers were exploited in spite of the efforts of the governments of India and Britain to protect them.

It was not surprising that the Franco-Mauritians should have behaved as they did. For one hundred years they and their ancestors had been accustomed to holding a privileged position and running the economy with slave labour. Legally slavery had been abolished. In practice, they began to operate a new labour system which some people felt was difficult to distinguish from slavery. The surprise was that the powerful forces in Britain which had, after a long struggle, outlawed slavery, should have allowed the planters to operate the new system. It is interesting to follow the conflicting interests of the opposing forces through the period from 1835 to the end of the century.

Those who had fought for abolition were well aware of the evils of the system of indentured labour. Lord Brougham, who found it difficult to draw the line between the old slavery and the new indentured labour, tried in 1838 to condemn the Indian Government's Order in Council of 1837 which had allowed the system to start. His resolution was rejected by the British House of Lords.[1] Later in the same year, speaking in a debate on a Bill for the protection of Indian emigrants, he denounced the system and pointed out some of its unacceptable conditions: 'Had not their Lordships seen the circular of the Messrs. Huson who held themselves forth as accomplished man merchants, and who bragged that in two years they could furnish to Mauritius

Hill coolies landing at Mauritius 1842

5000 hill coolies at ten pounds a head, including passage money, provision, water and all other stores and an advance of six months' wages and clothing, these wages being five rupees or about ten shillings a month, while the wages of a day labourer in England were, instead of three pence or four pence a day, from three shillings to four shillings a day; these poor and ignorant creatures, the hill coolies, were smuggled away under the idea that Mauritius to which they were going was a village belonging to the East India Company.'

Abuses and attempts at improvement

The Bill passed through the House of Lords; but the government of India was by now worried about reports of ill-treatment of Indian immigrants to Mauritius and of abuses of the system. The British House of Commons dropped the Bill. The government of India suspended emigration in 1839. Enquiries were held into the working of the system by committees of the governments of Bombay, Madras and Bengal and, at the request of the Indian government, by a commission set up by the Mauritian government. The Indian committees found much evidence that emigrants were deceived about conditions of work and about the whereabouts of Mauritius. Conditions aboard ship were often very bad: serious overcrowding, brutal treatment by ships' captains, disease and death were common. Many emigrants never received their promised six months' wages in advance. The local commission in Mauritius claimed that, generally, the conditions under which Indian immigrants lived and worked in Mauritius were satisfactory and that, in any case, they were superior to those in many parts of India. This last argument was a favourite line of defence by the

1 *The British system of government: Britain in the early nineteenth century was a constitutional monarchy. The King (or Queen) was Head of State but the real power of government, of making and executing laws, lay elsewhere. Parliament, the legislature, made laws. Parliament consisted of two 'houses'; the House of Commons whose members were elected, and the House of Lords whose members were hereditary peers or 'lords'. Parliamentary Bills become Acts and have the force of law after being passed by both the House of Commons and House of Lords and after finally receiving the 'royal assent'. This last stage of a Bill's passage into law had become little more than a formality by the mneteenth century.*

planters and their supporters.

One member of the commission, however, was very critical of the treatment of the immigrants. This was Mr Special Justice Anderson who wrote: 'With a few exceptions the immigrants were treated with great and unjust severity by overwork and by personal chastisement; their lodgings were either too confined and disgustingly filthy, or none were provided for them; and in case of sickness, the most culpable neglect was evinced in withholding the accommodation, advice and attendance which the utter helplessness of the sufferer so urgently required. None of the establishments had sufficient hospital accommodation, and the expense of the public hospital was always urged as an excuse for not sending them there. The Indians' prejudices were never considered. Their deplorable state of destitution was always urged as an argument in favour of their improved condition here, without any reference to the change which had taken place by their emigration from comparative idleness and indolence, with the full enjoyment of all their natural prejudices, to severe and unremitting labour under many painful restrictions; they were generally pillaged of the six months' pay advanced to them in India and were compelled to toil here for a recompense which bears no relation to the work to which they were subjected as compared with the common value of labour in the colony, or the sum they would have earned had they had the free disposal of their own time.' The evidence of this one member of the commission can hardly be reconciled with the report of the others and suggests that the whole exercise was meant to be a cover-up.

In spite of the evidence which pointed to the unsatisfactory nature of the system, emigration was permitted again by the Indian Government from the end of 1842. The only step taken to try to improve the system was the issue by the Colonial Office in 1842 of an Order in Council which laid down a set of regulations to control the traffic. These authorised the government of Mauritius to appoint emigration agents at Indian ports and the Indian Government to appoint a Protector of Immigrants in Mauritius.[2] Most of the regulations, however, were concerned with conditions on the voyage. There were also clauses which required the Protector to make sure that no labourer had been compelled to emigrate against his will, to allow Indians some part in the choice of their employer and to prevent them entering into a contract before they had been in Mauritius for forty-eight hours. The regulations were attacked as inadequate by members of the anti-slavery movement, but with no success.

The first Protector of Immigrants was Mr C. Anderson. He was anxious to restrict the recruitment and export of emigrants to Calcutta and its hinterland and officially this became the position in 1844. Mr Anderson's job was an unenviable one and he was under attack from the planters, who wanted more labourers, and from others in India who complained of continuing abuses. Thomas Hugon, who became Protector of Immigrants in 1847 and held the post until 1859, had good intentions and sympathy towards the immigrants and an understanding of them. But this was not enough to protect the Indians from the ruthlessness of the planters. Throughout Hugon's period of office, and for many years after it, the planters did their utmost to change the law in their own favour. In his *Sketch on Immigration* Hugon realised that, for the planters, the early years, 1834 to 1838, were the golden age of immigration. Amongst other things in that period the immigrants had been turned into virtual slaves on five years' contract. A return to a five-year contract was one of the main aims of the planters in the late 1840s and 1850s. By 1849 they had managed to make three years' service one of the conditions of the signing of a contract. By 1853 the earlier right of an immigrant to a free return passage had been whittled away with nothing to

2 *Protector of Immigrants: The regulation contained in the Order in Council (1842) gave to the Indian Government the power to appoint a Protector of Immigrants in Mauritius. In practice the Mauritian authorities seem to have appointed a Protector of Immigrants of their own before the Indian Government did so. Most Protectors were appointed in this way by the Mauritian authorities. Another official, the Protector of Emigrants, was appointed by the government in India to supervise the shipping of emigrants from Calcutta.*

compensate for it. By 1856 permission to recruit labourers had been extended from Calcutta to other Indian ports.

Only in one respect was there any attempt to improve conditions in these middle years of the nineteenth century. There was an attempt to increase the number of female and family emigrants. This was an aspect of the indentured labour system that was closely linked to the right to a return passage. Originally labourers were expected to emigrate alone, leaving behind their wives and families in India. It was then logical to expect that most would want to return to India after the completion of their contracts.

Having abolished the right to a free return passage the planters were at least honest enough to accept that it was reasonable that the numbers of male and female immigrants should be more equal. Moreover, to increase the number of women would increase the willingness of the men to stay on in Mauritius for a long time, which was one of the planters' basic objectives.

Immigration to Mauritius reached its peak between 1858 and 1859, a time when the demand for Mauritian sugar was also approaching its maximum. So urgent was the planters' need for more coolies that they were allowed to import them at their own expense and they began to send their own experienced workers to the emigration ports to try to persuade more Indians to emigrate. The disruption and disorder caused by the mutiny in India in 1857 made more people ready to emigrate.

In 1859 more than 44,000 were recruited from Calcutta, Madras and Bombay. The numbers emigrating from each port were approximately 23,000, 16,000 and 5000 respectively. Some of these recruits had already signed contracts with the agents of particular employers before leaving India. In this same year Nicholas Beyts replaced Thomas Hugon as Protector of Immigrants. He held the post for nearly twenty years during the period when the exploitation of the coolies became most intense. On the whole Beyts was less sympathetic to the interests of the labourers than Hugon had been and more ready to fall into line with the wishes of the employers.

Indian indentured labourers

Living and working conditions

Before looking at the period of greatest repression for the Indians, which followed the introduction of a new labour law in 1867, some attempt must be made to describe the conditions of life and work which most of them had to tolerate. Even before they had left India many of them were misled about their prospects by the agents who recruited them at the port of emigration. They were often given a quite false impression of the kind of work they were going to undertake and of the geographical position of Mauritius. They were told that the work was light and that the voyage was no longer than a few days. However, even if they had been told the truth about these two matters, most of the Indians would have still volunteered to emigrate. The economic condition of India was very difficult for the peasants. This was partly the result of the new system of land tax recently introduced by the British. This had disastrous consequences for Indians of all classes. Many landowners had been made bankrupt and many peasants had been thrown off the land and made destitute. Almost any prospect was better than that of staying in India at that time. An additional factor made some more ready than ever to leave their homeland. This was the period when reforms introduced by the British were beginning to make many Indians feel that their traditional way of life and culture were being threatened.

The last paragraph makes it clear that the motives which drove so many thousands of Indians to emigrate as indentured labourers in the period after 1840 were not always the same. Historians and economists talk about the 'push-pull' factors which operate in cases of large-scale movements of people. Sufficient has been written above to make it clear that amongst the 'pull' forces which attracted Indians to Mauritius were misleading, or even deliberately untrue, stories about the good life and the pleasant conditions that awaited them on arrival in Mauritius. There is disagreement about the 'push' forces which made many Indians anxious and ready to leave India and seek a new life elsewhere. Most writers favour the view that it was mainly the conditions of desperate poverty which prevailed in so many parts of India that were overwhelmingly the strongest and the commonest of these factors. An increasing number of Indian scholars, however, believe that another powerful 'push' factor lay in the desire of many Indians to escape the threat which they felt that British rule and British reforms posed to their culture and way of life. They decided to emigrate in order to preserve and spread their culture and be able to follow their traditional way of life without interference. There is also evidence that, in spite of regulations which tried to prevent it, various forms of compulsion were used by recruiting agents to persuade Indians to sign contracts as labourers.

The voyage

Whatever their reasons for emigrating, the next trial facing the labourers was the ocean voyage. This could last anything from five to twelve weeks according to the weather conditions. The detailed regulations laid down in the 1842 laws were seldom observed. Overcrowding was common and there were serious health risks in the cramped and insanitary quarters. Immigrants often had to spend long periods in quarantine when ships arrived carrying passengers who had infectious diseases. A scandal resulted from one such case in 1856. At the beginning of that year a ship carrying 272 passengers arrived off Mauritius. Twenty had died of cholera on the voyage. Another ship followed with 380 passengers of whom twenty-two had died. Both ships were ordered to Gabriel Island, a rocky inhospitable island to the north of Mauritius. Before the passengers were eventually allowed into Mauritius in May 1856, 273 had died of cholera, dysentery and fever. For nearly a year the Indian Government suspended emigration as a protest against what they regarded as gross neglect by the Mauritian authorities. The suspension came at a bad time for the planters as sugar production was being increased rapidly at the time.

Food was seldom both wholesome and plentiful and was frequently very inadequate and unpleasant. Severe punishments were often inflicted on emigrants and there were cases of beatings so severe that they caused deaths. Few immigrants arrived in Mauritius with their advance of six months' wages still intact.

Arrival

After being cleared by the medical authorities in Mauritius, life for the Indians began in the Port Louis depot. In theory, the immigrants were supposed to have some choice in their future employer. In theory also the Protector of Immigrants was supposed to be in charge of the activities in the depot. In practice the planters and their agents, the sirdars or overseers, usually bargained for the right to particular immigrants. Bribery played a large part in the proceedings. There were disorderly and sometimes violent scenes when the depot was full of newly arrived labourers.

Accommodation

After the depot the next stop for the indentured labourer was the estate camp, still often called the 'camps des noirs'. There was significance in the retention of the name from the period of slavery. The accommodation for the Indian coolie was no better than it had been for the slave. There were lines of thirty to forty rooms side by side and back to back, usually on one level. Cooking was done outside on a verandah. An official of the immigration department described the construction of the rooms early in the 1870s:

> the dwellings of the Indian labouring population are composed of light frames of rods the side covered with cane straw [trash] tied into bundles and sometimes plastered with a thin coating of mud, their average height being from four to five feet . . . I had to inspect the inside of these cottages on my hands and knees.[3]

This accommodation was meant to house a family or three male workers. Often as many as six men lived in one room. Medical facilities were totally inadequate even after 1900. Only fifteen doctors were available to look after the patients in estate hospitals serving a population of nearly 92,000 plantation workers.

Wages and discipline

Living in these conditions the Indian labourers faced six days a week from dawn till dusk in one of the hardest of physical jobs. It had been normal for slaves to be allowed a period to become acclimatised both to their new surroundings and to their new job. No such concession was made to the indentured labourers. They were being paid and had to earn their money, little though it was. Wages in Mauritius were lower than in most of the other sugar colonies and almost exactly half those in the Caribbean. The normal earnings were R5 (or 10/-) per month. It was argued that wages were supplemented by rations. Throughout the whole of the period from beginning to end of immigration (1834-1907) wages remained almost unchanged.

The planters argued that profits were marginal and wages had to be kept low. Since there were no incentives to encourage labourers to work hard they had to be made to work hard by the threat of punishment and a variety of penalties. Even with wages as low as they were, they were often paid weeks or even months in arrears. This was one of the workers' most common complaints. If planters were in financial difficulty their first way of trying to escape was to hold back wages.

Workers could be fined for a long list of 'offences'. The fines were simply held back from wages. The most notorious of all penalties operated in Mauritius was the 'double cut'. It was operated on many estates from the early days of the indenture system. It was made official by Ordinance 22 in 1847. If a worker was absent from work for one day, he lost two days' wages. Workers could frequently find themselves in debt at the end of a month and having to work for no wages the following month to pay off the fines. The practice survived until 1909.

Duties

Work on the sugar plantations was, like most agricultural jobs, seasonal. The busiest season was undoubtedly the harvest. It was relentless, heavy, unpleasant work. Once cut, the cane had to be transported without delay to the mill or factory for processing. Even in the so-called slack season, however, there was heavy work to be done in Mauritius. Workers were required to clear the land of the volcanic rock boulders and pile them up in great heaps between the cultivated patches. Whilst more land was being brought under cultivation to meet a growing demand this was a big task. Regular work on the estates was performed for six days of the week. It would be a mistake to regard Sunday as a day of rest. The 'corvée' was performed on Sundays in Mauritius. This was unpaid labour. Usually it entailed an additional, unpaid, day's work at the regular job in the fields.

Prejudice and repression

Given these conditions it was not surprising that Indians who had served out their period of indenture were reluctant to renew their contract. Some, in the days when a free return passage was available, returned to India. Others left the estates and the camps and sought a freer, better life either in a village or a town. Thomas Hugon, the Protector of Immi-

3 *From H. Tinker,* A New System of Slavery, *p. 207.*

grants, understood and sympathised with the Indians' desire to escape from estate life. He estimated that there were between 20,000 and 30,000 'free' Indians and that most of them led blameless and busy lives. However their peaceful behaviour and industrious habits were not appreciated. In the view of the planters, community Indians who either refused to renew their contracts or who tried to escape from their estates before their contracts expired became vagrants. Planters always hoped that indentured labourers would continue to work on the estates. They could not accept the obvious explanation that no indentured labourer wanted to sign on again because the conditions of life and work were so bad.

From the earliest days of the system, planters invented the idea that Indians were restless wanderers incapable of staying in any job for long and that they must be forced into better ways by new regulations. To strengthen the case for issuing new regulations, a second myth was spread by the planters, that Indians were careless about sanitation and cleanliness. They were blamed for most of the epidemics that broke out on the island in the nineteenth century.

In the 1860s a series of epidemics broke out, culminating in the most devastating of all in 1866-1867. It was later discovered that this was an outbreak of malaria, the first ever on the island. This epidemic, coupled with the alleged increase in cases of vagrancy, was the justification for the introduction of the new and repressive Labour Law of 1867.

The Indians find support

Attempts were made to argue that the law of 1867 was designed to protect the Indian labourer against the error of his own ways. This is a common trick practised by those who want to disguise what is, in fact, a repressive law. 'Old immigrants', that is those who had completed a term of contract labour, were obliged to register and to provide themselves with a ticket carrying a photograph. This was a form of pass and those who could not produce it on demand by a policeman or a magistrate were liable to arrest. The intention of the planters was to exert pressure on the Indians with a view to forcing more of them to remain on the estate. Many who had escaped and were doing other jobs were harassed under the new law.

The governor at the time was Sir Henry Barkly, a man with an interest in plantations in the Caribbean and sympathetic to the planters. The Inspector General of Police, Captain Blunt, was particularly zealous in applying the law and in 1869 over 30,000 Indians, one in five of the Indian population, were arrested for vagrancy. Vagrancy hunts were organised in much the same way as a hunting party might have been organised in the eighteenth century to hunt down runaway slaves. However, support for the down-trodden and exploited Indian labourer was at hand. In 1870, Governor Barkly was replaced by Sir Arthur Gordon, a man with very different views who had already shown sympathy with Indian labourers in Trinidad, in the Caribbean.

Adolphe de Plevitz

A year earlier the owner of the sugar plantation of Nouvelle Découverte in the hills behind Port Louis had begun to take up the cause of the Indians and to organise a petition. His name was Adolphe de Plevitz. He was a man of principle and liberal views and his own workers were free to come and go as they pleased. The petition of the 'Old Immigrants' was presented to Governor Gordon on 6 June 1871. It carried the signatures or marks of over 9000 Indians. The combination of de Plevitz's enthusiasm for the cause and Gordon's sympathetic attitude towards the Indians promised that something at last might be done to improve their position. De Plevitz followed up his petition with a pamphlet with the title *Observations on the Petition*. This appeared early in August.

The planters were furious with de Plevitz. They began a campaign of abuse and tried hard to discredit him. His German-sounding name gave them a useful weapon against him. The Franco-Prussian War[4] had just been fought and he was denounced as a Prussian spy. In fact he had been born in Paris and had fought in both the French and British armies. The planters petitioned for his expulsion, but for once the governor was not prepared to be a tool of the planters. De Plevitz was then physically attacked in the centre of Port Louis and, to add insult to injury, was charged with

Adolphe de Plevitz

disturbing the peace. Again the governor disallowed the charge. De Plevitz refused to be put off by hostile demonstrations. Gordon set up a commission of inquiry to look into the behaviour and practices of the police. The members of the commission were generally men with close links with the planters but one member, Judge Gurrie, had an independent mind and no fear of the planters. Largely through his dominating influence the report was critical of the police, the immigration department and of the way in which the law of 1867 was being applied.

New allies in India

Indirectly the cause of the indentured labourers found two new allies, and the system itself two outspoken critics. One was the new lieutenant-governor of Bengal, from where most of the emigrants sailed to the sugar colonies. This was Sir George Campbell and he began to tighten up the conditions under which coolies were recruited and transported to the colonies. The other was A.S. Hume who was responsible for emigration in the government of India. He also wanted to tighten up regulations at the Indian end of the system. He was shocked by the report of the police commission of inquiry, accused the Mauritian Protector of Immigrants of neglecting his duties and called for his resignation.

The Royal Commission of 1872

In the meantime in Mauritius both Governor Gordon and the planters, for different reasons, pressed for a Royal Commission to investigate the whole position of indentured labourers in Mauritius. The Colonial Secretary appointed two commissioners, W.E. Frere and V.A. Williamson. Both were barristers and they arrived in Mauritius to begin their enquiry in April 1872. Their work took eighteen months to complete and their report was not published until 1875.

It was a very thorough piece of work and included much historical background to the whole system of Indian indentured labour. The commissioners heard de Plevitz's own evidence and subjected him to close questioning. Though they were critical of de Plevitz's pamphlet and the tone in which it was written they nevertheless accepted that all his charges were well founded. The system and those who operated it were roundly condemned. The Inspector General of Police, Lieutenant-Colonel O'Brien, and the Protector of Immigrants, Mr Beyts, came in for special criticism. The commissioners found the title of 'Protector' a very misleading one. The enquiry revealed that although 5000 complaints had been made about wages alone, and many on other grounds, the Protector of Immigrants had initiated only one appeal on behalf of the

4 *Franco-Prussian War: a war fought in Europe between France and Prussia, 1870-71. The war was won decisively by Prussia and enabled Prussia to complete the process of uniting most of Germany around her and thus forming the German Empire. A 'Prussian' would thus be unpopular amongst Franco-Mauritians whilst the memory of France's defeat by Prussia was still fresh.*

immigrants. The report stated firmly that the commissioners had found no grounds for the passing of the Labour Law of 1867:

> We have in our report endeavoured impartially to examine the chief reasons alleged for the passing of the law, viz, the vagrancy, idleness and improvidence of the Indians, their inhumanity to each other during the epidemic, their filthy habits and their participation in the crime of *dacoitee* or gang robbery; we must here repeat our failure to detect anything so peculiar to the old immigrants not under indenture as to have warranted the stringent measures invoked against them by the public and enacted against them in an ordinance.

Recommendations

The report made a number of recommendations for changes in the regulations affecting indentured labourers and for effective action by the authorities. Amongst these were the abolition of compulsory work on Sundays, the introduction of more women immigrants to equalise the ratio between the sexes and the improvement of medical care on the estates. It also recommended that inspections should be regularly carried out and that the governor should be empowered to have immigrants withdrawn from bad estates or from those whose owners ignored the laws and regulations. However, the double cut was to stay as a justifiable system and the registration of immigrants at district police offices was to be continued. The Colonial Secretary made the comment that the power of enforcing the cut should be exercised only after due precautions had been observed.

By the time that the report was published several of the original actors in the drama had left the stage. Governor Gordon had resigned in 1874 and was replaced by Sir Arthur Phayre. Phayre was involved in the drafting and promotion of the new law and regulation of 1878. Adolphe de Plevitz, without whom the two commissions would not have been set up and the reform movement would not have started, was not even consulted about the new law. Most important of all, however, as their opponents disappeared, the planters remained firmly entrenched in their position of privilege on the island. They were very firmly of the view that they and their ancestors were the ones who had made Mauritius what it was and their interests were paramount. The British and the Indians, who were late-comers to the scene, were not going to dislodge them.

Different racial groups in Mauritius 1857

British governors came and went fairly quickly. They barely had the time to weigh up the situation in the island. The planters were permanent residents and their privileged position had been built up over generations. Even if a governor such as Gordon showed sympathy for the Indian labourer, the planters could afford to wait until a more pliable governor arrived. Apart from the governor, the judges and a few top officials, the administration was dominated by Franco-Mauritians and Creoles with a vested interest in the existing system.

The planters' counter-attack

On the publication of the Royal Commission's report the planters prepared to fight back. A committee of the Chamber of Agriculture, the body which represented the planters' interests and opinions, was set up to examine the report. To their own satisfaction its members found the report's condemnation of their position unacceptable. This was the beginning of their counter-attack. They fought some of the clauses in the new law, particularly the one which allowed the governor to remove indentured labourers from bad estates. Their opposition was successful and the clause was changed. In its new form the governor could act only against an employer who had been convicted of offences more than four times within two years.

The position of Indian labourers after 1878

After six years of enquiries, reports, despatches and drafting of new laws the planters' position was in practice as strong as ever and that of the immigrants was, for all practical purposes, as vulnerable as ever to exploitation and injustice. The long drawn-out events of the years 1869 to 1878 had demonstrated that the system erected by the planters in their interests could not be broken, even in the words of Professor Tinker, 'by a crusading governor' (Gordon). Sir George Campbell, commenting on the clause in the new law of 1878 about the governor's power to remove immigrants from bad estates, wrote: 'Very great firmness and very great capacity [on the part of the governor] to resist unpopularity are required, and very strong support from the Colonial Office when he does his duty, the contrary when he does not.' This combination of forces to resist the entrenched power of the planters was unfortunately not forthcoming. No governor ever used this particular power.

Long after he had left Mauritius, ex-governor Gordon expressed his opinion that the new law of 1878 had worked an enormous amount of good. It is true that the rigorous application of the 1867 law and the hunting down of Indians not working on the sugar estates had been ended by governors like Gordon and Phayre. Moreover in the last twenty years of the nineteenth century fewer Indians were living on the estates, which shows that increasing numbers were finding other kinds of employment. More and more of the flimsy homes of Indians were built alongside the island's roads. Many Indians found another way of escape from plantation work by buying smallholdings on many large estates when they were broken up. Indians ceased to be indentured labourers and increasingly became free labourers. Governor Gordon's ideal of a completely free labour force, however, was not achieved until the law of 1878 was finally replaced by a new one in 1922.

Other Indian immigrants

The indentured labourers were not the only Indians coming into Mauritius in the nineteenth century. As the indentured labourers began to arrive from the 1830s onwards a significant number of Indian traders followed to supply the needs of the rapidly increasing Indian population. These needs took two main forms: rice as the staple food and cotton cloth as the material for clothing. Both had to be imported in large and growing quantities. Most of these traders came from western India and sailed through Bombay. They were Gujarati speakers and Muslims by religion. Economically and socially they were of a different class from the more numerous labourers. They were also predominantly townsmen.

What Indians most lacked in the nineteenth century was a leader of real standing and ability, a spokesman and a champion to fight for an improvement in their position. Those who had taken up their cause so far were not Indian. The position changed early in the twentieth century. Gandhi called briefly at Mauritius in 1901 and was shocked to discover how his countrymen's interests were being neglected and how complete was the gulf between the Port Louis Indian traders and the labourers on the plantations. At the time Gandhi had more than a full-time job campaigning for the rights of Indians in South Africa. In 1907 he played a part in the decision of Manilal Doctor, a young Indian lawyer, to take up a practice in Mauritius. His activities on the island will be described in the next chapter.

Suggestions for revision

This chapter deals with the system of indentured labour, perhaps the most important single topic in the history of Mauritius.

You should know the main aspects of the system of indentured labour, including:

a) the methods of recruitment of Indian labourers and conditions on the voyage;
b) the reasons why so many Indians were willing to emigrate as indentured labourers;
c) the terms of their contracts, in theory and in practice;
d) the living and working conditions of the immigrants;
e) the way in which the Franco-Mauritians were able to exploit the Indian labourers, in spite of regulations to prevent this and the efforts of the governments of India and Britain to protect the workers;
f) the efforts made by Adolphe de Plevitz, Governor Gordon and others to improve the conditions for Indian immigrants.

You should also know about:

a) the work and importance of each of the following, all of whom were involved in some way with Indian immigrant workers: Thomas Hugon; Governors Barkly, Gordon and Phayre; and Adolphe de Plevitz;
b) the importance of the 'double cut';
c) the Labour Laws of 1867 and 1878 and the Royal Commission of 1872.

Suggestions for further work

1. In the nineteenth century, Indians went as labourers to many different parts of the world. Find out a) to which other places they went and b) what kind of work they did.
2. There is some argument about the motives which led Indians to emigrate in large numbers. Which of the motives do you think was the most important, and why?
3. Imagine that you were an Indian immigrant to Mauritius in the middle of the nineteenth century. Explain a) why you decided to emigrate; b) describe the voyage to Mauritius; and c) describe your life on the sugar estate in Mauritius where you eventually lived and worked.

CHAPTER 11

A related story: Chinese immigration

In the second half of the 19th century, China, like India, was compelled to come to terms with the necessities of British imperialism. This meant supplying its share of the manpower necessary for the exploitation of the British colonies. In Mauritius, the organized introduction of mass Indian indentured labour led to favourable conditions for the arrival of free Chinese traders and artisans. The Chinese settled near the large sugar estates, opening small shops initially to meet the needs of their indentured Indian brothers. The frequency of sea communication between Mauritius and India after 1850 greatly facilitated Chinese immigration to the island. Chinese immigrants were easily able to obtain a passage on ships transporting Indian indentured labourers from Calcutta to Mauritius. The British Indian Steam Navigation Company began, after 1850, to organise an increasing number of voyages between India and Mauritius.

Causes of Chinese emigration

Chinese immigration to Mauritius began towards the end of the 18th century and became a steady flow which gradually gained momentum in the nineteenth century. At that time, emigration from China constituted a crime sanctioned by the death penalty, and the first migrants were careful to conceal their country of origin and the circumstances in which they left their country.

During the first half of the 19th century, Chinese society was undergoing a massive upheavel. In particular the Treaty of Nanking (1842) which declared Canton to be an open port considerably increased population pressure on an already crowded city. Economic recession, famine, and unemployment drove a large part of the surrounding rural population towards the city. Hardest hit were members of the trading class whose businesses suffered on account of the heavy toll levied on the transfer of their goods to market towns both by the government and by "Triad" organisations in areas under their control. One of the consequences of this situation was the increase, after 1845, of Chinese immigrants from the merchant class. By the end of the century they formed the vast majority of Chinese settlers in Mauritius.

The development of the Chinese 'boutique' in the 19th century

As we have already seen, the intro-duction of Indian indentured labour enabled Chinese shopkeepers to provide goods and services to this class of customers. Sugar cane cultivation was divided into 2 seasonal periods: Harvest season, known as 'la coupe' when the rhythm of work was very fast and employment plentiful; and the planting season, or 'l'entre-coupe' when only a minimum amount of labour was required to maintain the fields in good condition. During this period, many labourers were out of work and had to face very hard times as no state-run unemployment benefit schemes existed as yet.

The Chinese shopkeeper organised a system of credit sale which villagers called the 'roulement', a term which vividly expressed the tempo of life on sugar estates. This enabled labourers to purchase food on the strength of a promisory note drawn by the shopkeeper himself, and greatly contributed to relieving the plight of unemployment during the 'entre-coupe' season. This relationship was based on a feeling of mutual trust indicating that the Chinese shopkeeper was already a respected figure in the village.

The successful development of Chinese retail trading was, of course, partly based on their skill and hard work. But it was also due to the close-knit family spirit that existed among the first immigrants. Older members helped newcomers set up in business, raising funds through a lottery system and providing goods on credit which enabled new arrivals to make up an initial stock of merchandise. As Huguette Ly Thio Fane Pineo has put it, "credit sales was thus the link that bound the customer to the Chinese retailer and the Chinese retailer to the Chinese wholesaler. It became the motive power operating the economic progression of the community."[1]

However, economic progress rarely meant the making of big fortunes. Generally, in fact, members of the Chinese community have tended to move out of retail trade as soon as they have acquired other skills. While, in 1901, 81% of Chinese immigrants were traders, this figure fell to 33% in 1944, and to 20% in 1985.

Family structure of the Chinese community

Between 1760 and 1920 several attempts were made to use Chinese indentured labourers in Mauritius. None of these attempts proved successful primarily because agents found themselves unable to persuade Chinese women to accompany the migrants beyond the seas. Social customs prevailing in China did not allow the bride to accompany her husband overseas and until 1881 only 9 women had immigrated from China.

As a result, only a small proportion (8%) of Chinese traders were 'legally' married – i.e. according to British law – by the end of the 19th century. Most of the others were happy to co-habit with local women in keeping with Chinese custom which allowed a man to have as many concubines as he could financially support. Those who found themselves with a 'double' family suffered financial problems as they felt obliged to support members of the family left in China and to visit them as often as possible. Huguette Ly Thio Fane Pineo notes that in these situations, the wife left behind in China showed little grief at being without her husband for she was brought up to believe that the primary duty of a married woman was to serve her parents-in-law.

It was in the education of the children that a happier blend of Chinese and Mauritian culture was realised. While the father ensured that his children, particularly his sons, were raised in the traditional Chinese way of life and taught the Chinese language, the Christian mother brought the Roman Catholic faith to her children. As a result, the number of Catholics in the Chinese community increased rapidly during the first two decades of the 20th century. By 1920 the Chinese community was large enough to form a distinct ethnic group. They began to build social centres or 'pagodas', in the places where they had settled, on the model prevailing in their villages of origin.

At the same time, a more exclusively Chinese orientation towards family and social life began to emerge. The immigration of more young women from China was encouraged and some women took upon themselves the task of 'professional marriage makers', specializing in the 'importation' of brides. Mixed marriages within the community were now discouraged on the grounds that Mauritian women were not suitable for the kind of life that would be expected of them. Open mixing with the local population was also limited through the creation of exclusive associations such as the 'Chinese Nationality Club' (1925). Specialschools were created to foster a sense of Chinese national pride and the 'San Min Chu I' of Sun Yat-Sen became the foundation of the school curriculum. Ly Thio Fane Pineo notes that "the tendency towards the formation of a community impermeable to all external influence was encouraged by the five principles of the Chinese Nationalist

1 *Huguette Ly Thio Fane Pineo, Chinese Diaspora in western Indian Ocean (E.O.I., 1985) p. 80.*

party strongly supported by overseas Chinese".[1] These five elements according to Sun Yat-Sen's principles were blood, language, mode of life, religion and customs, which needed to be preserved and transmitted unimpaired.

Integration of the Chinese community

During the Second World War, Mauritius played a crucial role in supporting the war effort of the Allies. The strategic role of the island was enhanced after 1942 when the Japanese overran South East Asia and began to exercise authority over the eastern part of the Indian Ocean. China's defeat and occupation by Japan had a profound impact on the Chinese community in Mauritius who had actively supported Chiang Kai-Shek's war efforts. In general, the Chinese community were opposed to the establishment of the communist régime in China, and this widened the gulf with the mother country. They now began to realise that Mauritius offered them the hope of a secure future, especially as the reconstruction programme inspired by the British Labour Government promised to bring to an end the war-time hardships and restrictions. With the achievement of Mauritian independence in 1968, the Chinese community seized the opportunity to actively contribute to the creation of a Mauritian nation.

Suggestions for revision

This chapter deals with the arrival and settlement of Chinese traders, an important aspect of the peopling of Mauritius.

You should know:

a) The causes of Chinese emigration.
b) The origins and development of the Chinese shop.
c) the reason for the failure of Chinese indentured labour.
d) Changes in attitudes towards ethnic identity and marriage.

Suggestions for further work

1 In the nineteenth century, Chinese people migrated to many different parts of the world. Find out (a) to which other places they went and (b) what kind of work they did.
2 What do you think were the similarities and differences between Chinese and Indian emigration?

1 *Huguette Ly Thio Fane Pineo, Chinese Diaspora in western Indian Ocean (E.O.I., 1985) p. 289*

CHAPTER 12

Developments in Port Louis and the political life of Mauritius between 1810 and 1922

The last two chapters have been concerned with the growth of the sugar industry and the Indian immigrants, most of whom worked in that industry. In this chapter we shall return to the story of the capital, Port Louis, still the only important urban centre in 1810; and to the politics and government of the island.

Cyclones, epidemics and health measures

The story of Port Louis has been told in Auguste Toussaint's book, *Port Louis, A Tropical City*, in some detail. Here the main features of the story will be summarised. Throughout the nineteenth century Port Louis continued to be afflicted by the two different kinds of disasters to which its inhabitants had become accustomed: cyclones and epidemics. These inevitably affected adversely its growth and development. Cyclones caused large-scale destruction of property, particularly of the poorer houses, and of crops. Epidemics brought sudden changes in population and acted as a brake on population growth. Cyclones struck frequently and the most destructive in the nineteenth century were those in the following years: 1818, 1819, 1824, 1844, 1848, 1865, 1868, 1879, 1884 and 1892. Only in the 1830s and the 1850s was Mauritius spared the setbacks that were caused by bad cyclones.

Outbreaks of epidemic disease were equally frequent. Smallpox, which had been the most serious menace in the eighteenth century, became less of a threat in the nineteenth. An

Cyclone damage in Port Louis, April 1892

outbreak in 1811 was checked quickly but another in 1891 spread rapidly as a result of some negligence on the part of the authorities at a time when they were beginning to believe that the disease was a thing of the past. It claimed over 650 victims before it was controlled. Cholera occurred more frequently. The first outbreak was in 1819 and others followed in 1856, when over 33,000 people died, in 1859 and in 1861. There was a single outbreak of rabies in 1813 which was checked by the drastic step of slaughtering all the island's dogs. A serious epidemic of influenza in 1893, the first in Mauritius, caused over 500 deaths, and there were further epidemics in 1906 and 1919. In the last of these, when influenza was common throughout the world, 4000 people died in Mauritius. In 1899 the old-fashioned plague visited the island for the first time. It was particularly persistent and reached epidemic proportions annually until 1917 with a final serious outbreak in the year 1921 to 1922.

Most serious of all, however, in its long-term effects was malaria. The island was free of the disease until 1865 when it was introduced, probably from East Africa, though, as usual, the blame for its appearance was placed upon the Indians. It raged until 1868 by which time it had killed over 30,000 people. At first it was known simply as the 'Mauritian disease' because it was not identified for some time. It then remained endemic on the island until stamped out by a massive campaign of eradication started in 1953 (see Chapter 16).

Serious outbreaks of killer diseases such as these emphasise that Mauritius, in spite of its geographical isolation, was no longer isolated. It was visited annually by large numbers of ships from all parts of the world. The arrival of every ship was a potential hazard to health in the days before routine and reliable health checks. All the diseases mentioned were introduced from outside. The authorities were slowly made more aware of the need for better health services, supplies of fresh, clean water and effective provision for drainage and the safe disposal of sewage. Awareness of the need, unfortunately, did not lead to quick action. The question of the water supply to Port Louis was tackled several times between 1820 and the end of the century but the problem was not solved in the nineteenth century. The safety and the quantity of the supply were both below standard until very recent times. The problem of sewage and drainage was first considered soon after the malaria epidemic of 1866 to 1868. At that time, people thought that the disease lay dormant in the soil, and there was such violent opposition to the idea of digging drains that the government dropped the scheme. It was not revived until the last decade of the nineteenth century and even then the authorities got no further than approving a scheme. A little work was carried out between the two World Wars, but the problem was not effectively tackled until after the Second World War.

Changes in population

The population of Port Louis at the beginning of the British period was about 24,000. By 1851 it had doubled and was just under 50,000. In the next ten years it had reached just about 75,000, the highest figure in the nineteenth century. A decline then began. By the beginning of the 1890s it was about 60,000; in 1901, 53,000; and in 1911, and again in 1921, just over 50,000. The rise in the first sixty years of the century is explained to a large extent by immigration. Most of the Indian traders, for example, who came to the island along with the indentured labourers after 1835 settled in Port Louis. Nearly two-thirds of the increase between 1851 and 1861 was accounted for by Asian immigrants, mainly Muslim traders from India. Before this influx of Asians the bulk of the inhabitants of Port Louis were Creoles, many of them employed as dock workers or in fishing. Port Louis, like many seaports, was becoming a cosmopolitan place where people of many different ethnic groups lived and worked and many others passed through while ships were loaded and unloaded.

The decline in the population of Port Louis after the mid-1860s was largely caused directly or indirectly by the epidemics already mentioned. The outbreak of a serious epidemic usually caused a panic exodus. During the cholera epidemic of 1819, for example, it was estimated that nearly 10,000 people left the town. An exodus like this was usually temporary. After the onset of malaria in 1865, however, it was different. The 1860s proved to be something of a disaster for Port Louis. Cholera epidemics in the opening years were followed by malaria, which had carried off over 18,000 people in Port Louis alone by 1868. In addition a bad cyclone made about 50,000 people homeless in the same year. Many of the wealthier inhabitants decided that the health risk of living in the capital was too high. They began to move out of the town onto higher ground further inland, especially into the Plaines Wilhems district.

It happened that the island's first railways had just been opened: the Northern line in 1864 and the Midland line in 1865. The latter, in particular, made it possible for the well-to-do to live in the healthier upland area whilst travelling to work in Port Louis. The population of Port Louis fell from about 75,000 before the malaria epidemic started to little more than 50,000 in 1918. At the same time the population of Plaines Wilhems rose from about 30,000 to over 70,000. This movement of population introduced a new and less desirable feature into the life of the island. In Port Louis the different ethnic elements in the population tended to have their own quarters where most of them lived. They nevertheless mingled naturally and freely with one another in going about their business. In the upland suburbs they were much more segregated than before. Curepipe, for example, was the favourite area for Franco-Mauritians and Rose Hill for the richer members of the coloured community. It is important to remember, however, that this was in no way the result of any official policy.

Changes in trade

The fortunes of Port Louis as a port fluctuated considerably during the nineteenth century. We have seen how, at the beginning of the century, the brisk trade of Port Louis was the result of the goods brought in by the corsairs and sold largely to merchants from neutral countries. This ended with the beginning of the effective British blockade after 1806. The British conquest brought only a slow revival, in spite of Governor Farquhar's efforts to stimulate trade by making Port Louis a 'free' port. A much more dramatic boost to trade resulted from Britain's decision to reduce duty on imported sugar from Mauritius to the same level as that from the Caribbean islands. From that date the trade of Port Louis expanded with the rapid growth of the sugar industry. This continued until the demand for Mauritian sugar began to decline after the mid-1860s. In the same period the volume of trade passing through Port Louis was further stimu-

The Central Railway Station, Port Louis, 1892

lated by the large quantities of food and clothing imported from India to meet the needs of the Indian immigrants. The number of ships calling at Port Louis reached its highest figure for the nineteenth century in the 1850s. There were 470 in 1850 and almost twice the number, 825, and more than twice the tonnage, in 1858.

The last figure was never again exceeded in the nineteenth century. Sugar exports were at their maximum in the mid-1860s. The opening of the Suez Canal in 1869 probably had only a small impact initially on the traffic calling at Port Louis. The switch from sailing ships to steamships which was taking place at the same time was another factor that, on balance, led to a more significant decline in ships using Port Louis. The harbour and docks were built with sailing ships in mind and the port was slow to adapt to the needs of the steamship era in matters like repair facilities. Additions to the facilities made as late as the 1850s were still not forward-looking enough and were soon out of date. In the long run the opening of the Suez Canal route and the switch from sail to steam together increased the isolation of Port Louis and diminished its trade.

Port Louis municipality 1850

In 1850 Port Louis was given a special status as a municipality. When the British took over the government of the island in 1810 they had set up a number of local communes to take the place of the local councils of the revolutionary period. These did not survive long and were dissolved in 1821 after some of them showed too much readiness to question the governor's orders and decisions. The Port Louis municipality set up in 1850 came in for much criticism, some of it probably deserved, as many matters of great importance to the town were neglected. It was, nevertheless, the most democratic institution on the island for most of the nineteenth century.

Politics and Government in Mauritius

Conflict between Government and planters

Political control in Mauritius from the beginning of the period of British rule was, in theory, in the hands of the governor who was in turn responsible to the Colonial Secretary and the British Government in London. Already, however, enough has been written to suggest that the governor's power was, in practice, far from absolute. The French settlers had been firmly established in the economic and social life of the island for too long to make it possible for the British authorities to take decisions which might harm the planters' interests and threaten to undermine their privileged position. This was particularly the case in any matter that affected the running of their estates. The system of indentured labour was established some time after the beginning of

Port Louis about 1850

British rule. It replaced the system of slave labour which the British Government had ended in Mauritius in 1835, but only after the planters had won their right to compensation. It was a system which served the interests of the planters as well as, if not better than, that of slave labour which it replaced. The planters showed on many occasions that regulations which were against their interests and which they opposed were difficult to introduce, easy to circumvent and almost impossible to enforce.

Governors of Mauritius who wanted a trouble-free life usually followed the path of least resistance and avoided conflict with the Franco-Mauritian planters. Occasionally this could lead to trouble with the British Government as Governor Gomm discovered when he sent a new ordinance approved by the planters to the Colonial Secretary, Lord Grey, in 1846. It was rejected on the grounds that its provisions were too harsh.

On the other hand some governors were not afraid to resist the planters. Sir Arthur Hamilton Gordon was one of them. He took issue with the planters over the delicate matter of the old immigrants and the planters made his life on the island so difficult and unpleasant that eventually he was driven to resign his post. Governor Sir William Nicolay in the 1830s who started his period of office by being tough with the planters over the Jeremie affair retreated from this line eventually. He abandoned Jeremie to his inevitable fate of being expelled for a second time when the Procureur Général angered the Franco-Mauritians by trying to rig the trial of the five men of Mahébourg whom he had arrested by replacing the regular judges of the Supreme Court with his own supporters. British officials, whether governors or lesser men, who came into direct conflict with the interests of the planters seldom came off best.

The constitutional position 1810-1885

What of the constitution? Initially under British colonial rule the governor's absolute power was not limited by any institution on the island. The governor worked through his officials who were all responsible to him. The old institutions that came into being in the French revolutionary period, like the Colonial Assembly, had been swept away by Decaen. The British had no intention of reviving them.

The Council of Government and the Colonial Committee

In 1825 under Governor Cole the British made a small but meaningless concession. A Council of Government was set up but merely consisted of the leading colonial officials through whom the governor was already carrying on his administration. These were the Chief Justice, the Chief Secretary, the Commanding Officer of the Garrison and the Controller of Customs. The leading members of the Franco-Mauritian community had to make use of a philosophical and intellectual organisation, the Oval Table, to air their views. Through Adrien d'Epinay, one of their leading members and a lawyer, they continued to press for a more official voice in the government of the island. Having failed to get this in 1825, they set up two years later, on their own initiative but with Governor Cole's approval, a Colonial Committee. The members were delegates from the various districts of the island representing the planters. They acted as watch-dogs of the interests of their class at a time when these were felt to be under increasing threat from the campaign being conducted in Britain for the abolition of slavery.

It was the Colonial Committee which sent Adrien d'Epinay to London as its spokesman in 1830 and again between 1833 and 1834 to press for the payment of compensation when slavery was abolished. The success of this mission has already been described (see Chapter 8). Adrien d'Epinay's mission had another objective. He was pressing for a change in the constitution which would give the Franco-Mauritians a place on the Council of Government, so far monopolised by officials. In this he had only limited success. In 1832, under Governor Sir Charles Colville, some changes were made in the composition of the council. It was to consist of fourteen members in all. Seven of them were to be colonial officials, ex-officio members.[1] The other seven

1 *Ex officio members: those who are automatically entitled to be members of a committee or other body because of the office or position they hold.*

Sir John Pope Hennessy

were to be nominated by the governor. In practice they were all members of the European community. This did not satisfy the Franco-Mauritians who would have liked the right to elect their own representatives on the Council of Government.

No further changes were made in the constitution until 1885. This did not mean, however, as the events of the intervening fifty years showed very clearly, that the planters were without influence or that their interests were neglected. The Chamber of Agriculture, established in 1853 and controlled by the planters, proved to be a very powerful and effective pressure group. Between 1835 and 1885 the position of the planters in relation to their indentured labourers was strengthened in the face of the British and Indian governments, both officially supposed to be concerned about the interests of the Indian labourers.

The Reform Movement and the Constitution of 1885

The only further change in the system of government between 1885 and 1922 came during the governorship of Sir John Pope Hennessy (1883-1889). Two Mauritian barristers, William Newton and Virgile Naz, were the leading figures in a campaign which was known as the Reform Movement. They were staunch supporters of the dominant planter community and Newton had represented it before the Royal Commission of 1872. They were themselves plantation owners and it would be a grave mistake to think of them as liberals or men anxious to promote democratic government in Mauritius. Their aim was to acquire for their own class more power in government through a more direct share in the election of the unofficial members of the Council of Government.

After their initial request to the Colonial Secretary had been turned down they succeeded in 1884 in winning the sympathy and support of Governor Pope Hennessy. Once this had been gained the only question that remained to be decided was the qualification for the franchise. The conservative views of Newton and Naz now emerged clearly. They were determined to fix a high property qualification. They were opposed by a group known as the 'democrats' who favoured a lower qualification. The supporters of Newton and Naz were known as the 'oligarchs' since they wished to restrict the right to vote to the very rich. In effect two political parties opposed each other over the franchise issue. A compromise which satisfied neither was finally imposed by the governor, but it still meant that only the rich would have the right to vote. These were predominantly white but not entirely so. Newton himself was a Creole and other rich Creoles qualified. He stood for election to the Council in the first election after the changes but failed to be elected.

The number of members in the Council of Government was increased from fourteen to twenty-seven. The new Council consisted of eight official members, nine nominated members, at least one-third of whom must hold no public office in the colony; and ten elected unofficial members, one from each rural district and two from Port Louis. The franchise was so restricted that even as late as 1936 only 3000 of the 56,000 inhabitants of Port Louis had the right to vote. It was in practice almost impossible for any but a white to be elected. In the first election in 1886 no Indian was elected. Pope Hennessy was so conscience-stricken by the fact that a quarter of a million Indians had no directly elected representative on the Council that he included an Indian amongst the nine nominated members.

The struggle for Indian rights

The conflict between 'oligarchs' and 'democrats' became more bitter during the remainder of the nineteenth century and into the first years of the twentieth century. In 1905 the two groups were formally organised into political parties. The party of the 'democrats' led by Dr Eugène Laurent was known as L'Action Libérale and their opponents as the Parti de l'Ordre. Dr Laurent, who was the mayor of Port Louis, was not a Franco-Mauritian. He came from the elite of the Creole community.

In 1907 an Indian barrister, Manilal Doctor, largely at the suggestion of Mahatma Gandhi, came to Mauritius to practise. He was shocked by the lack of rights, including political rights for Indians. He became a member of the Action Libérale Party. He tried to stir the Indian community out of its apathy and encourage its members to be active in politics. His efforts met with little response. In 1909 another Royal Commission, the Swettenham Commission, enquired into conditions on the island. Its terms of reference were wide and it looked at the political and economic situation in general. One of its specific tasks was to enquire into the position of Indians. Its conclusion was that 'One of the most difficult problems which lie before the Mauritius Government is that of its relations with the population of Indian descent. For about three-quarters of a century it has been found possible for the Colonial Government to regard the Indian as a stranger among a European civilisation, a stranger who must indeed be protected from imposition and ill-treatment and secured in the exercise of his legal rights, but who has no real claim to a voice in the ordering of the affairs of the Colony.' It recommended in its report that Indians should be represented in the Council of Government and that the indenture system should be ended.

Feeling ran high between the Action Libérale and the Parti de l'Ordre and serious rioting broke out in January 1911 at the time of the election. The disturbances in Port Louis were particularly violent. Much damage was done to property, mainly that belonging to oligarchs, and several people were killed. Only the outbreak of the First World War dampened down political tension. Yet an enquiry into the disturbances found that Indians had played no part in them and absolved them from any blame.

One of the ideas put forward by Manilal Doctor during his stay in Mauritius was that Mauritius should be linked politically with India. It is interesting to note that the Royal Colonial Institute (now the Royal Commonwealth Society) was also thinking along similar lines on the grounds that the Indian market for Mauritian sugar would be profitable to Mauritius. On the other hand, some Franco Mauritians after the First World War started a campaign for the restoration of Mauritius to France. It was called the Retrocession Movement. One of the reasons put forward in support of retrocession was the danger that French culture would be swamped by the Indian majority. The Movement was also stimulated and encouraged by the prominence given at the Versailles peace talks to the principle of self-determination, though in fact the logical application of this principle would have been to link the island with India with which the great majority of its inhabitants had cultural ties.

In fact there was little support for the movement even amongst the Franco-Mauritians. Its supporters nevertheless made it an election issue in 1921. The voters' verdict was decisive. Not a single Retrocession candidate was elected. The idea was killed stone dead. The deeper issues of the franchise and the rights of the Indian majority were, however, still just below the surface. Once the short-lived post-war economic boom had given way to the harsh conditions of the 1930s, discontent emerged again and Mauritian politics entered a new and more stormy phase.

Suggestions for revision

On the history of Port Louis you should know:

a) the main developments in the history and growth of Port Louis as a port and an administrative and residential centre;
b) the effect of epidemics and cyclones on the city's development;
c) the effect of transport changes on the development of the city.

On the political life you should know:
a) the main facts about the constitution and the system of government under the British, including the few changes that were made or attempted during this period, particularly the new constitution of 1885;
b) how and why the Franco-Mauritians dominated the political life of Mauritius;
c) about the work and importance of the following: Governors Farquhar, Colville, Nicolay and Pope Hennessy; Adrien d'Epinay; William Newton and Virgile Naz; Manilal Doctor and Eugène Laurent;
d) the importance of the following: the Council of Government; the Chamber of Agriculture; the municipality of Port Louis; the Constitution of 1885; the Royal Commission of 1909 (Swettenham Commission); and the Retrocession Movement.

Suggestions for further work

1 One of the keys to understanding the political, as well as the economic, life of Mauritius during the period 1810-1922 lies in a knowledge and understanding of the means by which the Franco-Mauritians managed to dominate both. Make a list of a) the main institutions through which this group exercised power and influence and b) the main occasions when they managed to preserve their dominant influence and successfully resisted change that would have undermined their influence and control.

2 Make sure you know the meaning of the following words: democrat, oligarch (page 71) and retrocession (page 72).

CHAPTER 13

The plural society of Mauritius

It wouid be appropriate at this point to take a closer look at the composition of Mauritian society. By 1922 the population of Mauritius had been built up since the arrival of the first settlers in the seventeenth century as the result of two main processes. Firstly there had been a steady influx of immigrants from other lands. This flow ended in the early 1920s with the last significant batch of Indian immigrants. Secondly the resident population had added to its numbers by the natural increase resulting from the excess of births over deaths. The first of these processes brought into Mauritius peoples of diverse origin, mainly from Europe, Madagascar, East Africa, India and China. This alone ensured that Mauritius would have a multi-racial and multi-cultural society. The second process has greatly increased the diversity of Mauritian society as a result of the intermarriage amongst the different groups of immigrants. The great majority of people of mixed race are called Creoles and add a further element of diversity to an already multi-cultural population.

Ethnic composition

The present day plural society of Mauritius is a complex one. It is possible to identify certain sections of the population on ethnic grounds. There is a very small but influential European section (about 1.3 per cent), a very large Indian section (about 65 per cent), and a small Chinese section (about 3 per cent). The remaining 30 per cent are largely Creoles of mixed ethnic origin (see below). It would be misleading, however, to regard these ethnic or community groups as being solid and indivisible. Cutting across the ethnic differences which distinguish and separate each of these sections from the others there are other factors which create divisions within each section. The Europeans, though mainly French in origin, include some British and a sprinkling of other nationalities. The Indians came originally from different parts of the sub-continent which has recently been divided into two modern states; India and Pakistan. Indo-Mauritians today have vague and arguably decreasing loyalties to one or other of these states according to their district of origin. The Indo-Mauritians are also divided on religious lines into Hindu and Muslim and further divided on linguistic lines. There are five important linguistic groups amongst them, together with several minor groups. The Chinese are divided by religion into those who are Christians and those who are not. Finally there are class divisions within each ethnic community which some would argue are as important as any of the others and which cut across ethnic, linguistic and religious divisions.

Diversity and unity

To claim today that there are occupational divisions which coincide with ethnic divisions is increasingly rash. There is more mobility of labour than at any previous time in Mauritian history. Nevertheless certain jobs still go with certain community groups to a degree which makes it worthwhile to identify the links. What is certainly true is that there is a real danger of exaggerating the importance of the ethnic divisions in the modern population of Mauritius. There are other factors which may, for some individuals and in certain circumstances, be more important. It is also worth remembering that those Mauritians who are called 'Creoles' are not an ethnic group. Almost by definition they are a mixture of two or more ethnic groups and in modern Mauritius many Creoles have the blood of several ethnic groups running in their veins. Creoles are not easily identified by physical appearance. Thus there are several divisive or diversifying factors in Mauritian society. To call these divisive is to imply that they are a bad or harmful influence

A Mauritian family

and that they do not make the task of nation building an easy one. To call them diversifying factors carries no such implication. In fact it implies rather that they are desirable features of society. This is true, however, only if their divisive influence can first be brought under control and all members of society can live in harmony and regard themselves as Mauritians first and members of some smaller community second.

Unifying influences

Language

Before considering these divisive or diversifying elements more fully it is necessary to balance the overall picture of Mauritian society by noting that there are unifying forces at work also. The languages spoken by different ethnic groups have already been mentioned. There are two main languages, however, which act as unifying, not divisive influences. The first of these is Creole, a language evolved originally by the Creoles, a people of mixed blood. Because it was a hybrid language, a language associated with no particular ethnic group, it has eventually become the language of almost all groups. It is based largely on French with a very definite local flavour popularised initially by African and Malagassy slaves or freed men and later by generations of Creoles. Almost all Mauritians understand it. In addition, in the rural areas, Bhojpuri is also widely used and understood even by non-Hindi speaking people.

Although French is more widely used than English (all the main daily newspapers are in French), English is the second unifying language, for different reasons and in a different way. It is the only language, apart from Creole, which is not associated with any ethnic group living in significant numbers on the island. Because Britain ruled the island for over 150 years it is the official language and it is the main language of education at secondary level and above.

Absence of segregation

Another important factor which has helped to avoid the development of tension between ethnic groups has been the absence in Mauritius of any system of legalised residential segregation. In practice communities of different ethnic groups have become established in different parts of the island. But this has arisen from the natural tendency for such groups to live together and not from any legally imposed regulation. People of different ethnic groups are free to live where they choose. The main constraints which limit choice are financial. Mauritius is not plagued, like many African countries, by the problem of ethnic groups occupying well-defined territorial areas.

Geographical factors

Finally the main geographical features of Mauritius have a unifying influence. Mauritius, being a small island, has in the surrounding ocean a boundary recognised by all. It is also a small crowded island with one of the highest population densities in the world. It would quickly become intolerable if, in such an environment, people did not live together in reasonable harmony.

Divisive influences

Ethnic origins and characteristics

We must now return to examine more closely

those features of Mauritian society which make it one of the world's most striking examples of a plural society. The signs of diversity are immediately visible: different physical types; different dress; different languages; different places of worship. In spite of the danger of exaggerating the importance of ethnic elements in the diversity, it is most convenient to consider Mauritian society in its four main community groups, three of which are ethnically based; the Europeans, the Indians, the Chinese. The fourth group, the Creoles, as already pointed out, is ethnically mixed.

The Europeans Today the Europeans form the smallest of the four groups. The European population fell after 1948 from about 26,000 to less than half that number but has since risen again. The great majority of these are of French descent and their influence is still very great. The Franco-Mauritians dominate the sugar industry and other fields of business such as commerce, trade and tourism. One of the remarkable facts about Mauritius is that the French, in spite of their defeat by the British in 1810, have continued to wield more influence in the business and cultural life of the island than the British. The explanation of this lies in the generous terms offered by the British to the French in 1810 (see Chapter 8). Their property, their language, their laws and their religion were all guaranteed and many of the French stayed on in the island under British control. The great majority of those who stayed were solid middle or upper-class French families already well established in the island's economic and social life. The Franco-Mauritians came from respectable families in France, many of them from Brittany. They have, if anything, remained more determined than their counterparts in France to preserve the gracious, cultured, affluent way of life of their forebears. They have lived in fine colonial-style houses in beautiful grounds in some of the choicest residential areas like Curepipe and Floréal. When the long period of Anglo-French warfare ended in 1810 many of the misfits and the less respectable elements of French society left the island. One of the great professions of the war years, that of privateering, disappeared from the area with the establishment of British dominance and control in the Indian Ocean. The other important feature of the Franco-Mauritians is that they are predominantly Roman Catholics.

From 1810 until independence (1968) the British supplied the personnel for the top administrative, judicial and military posts on the island. Few British came to settle and few entered business mainly because these areas were already firmly controlled by the Franco-Mauritians. Because English is the main language of education its influence is bound to increase, yet French, rather than English, has so far remained the language of those islanders whose education has gone beyond the primary level. With the introduction of free secondary education and the use of English in education at this level, the position is likely to change in the future. The prestige value of English is related to its role as the symbol of Western-style education.

The Sino-Mauritians The Sino-Mauritians from another small community within Mauritius. They are more numerous than the Europeans. Chinese minorities everywhere tend to keep together and preserve their identity, hence the existence in so many big cities all over the world of 'Chinatown' districts. Port Louis has its Chinatown or Chinese quarter

A Buddist temple at Port Louis

and in 1972 nearly 13,000 Chinese lived there. They are mainly urban dwellers because so many of them are retail traders and shopkeepers. They own and run small shops throughout the island and some large ones in the main towns. A substantial number also operate in the tailoring and food trades whilst many young Chinese find employment with banks and business firms. They are very hardworking, both at school and in their occupations, and a high proportion of Chinese are keen to obtain higher education. The Chinese were amongst the last of the main groups to come to Mauritius and did not begin to arrive in the island in significant numbers until about 1840.

The Indo-Mauritians The Indo-Mauritian community is the largest in the island, constituting some two-thirds of the total. In 1835, when slavery was abolished on the island, there were comparatively few Indians in Mauritius. Those who were already there were mainly traders or people with some skill as artisans. The great build-up of the Indian element in the Mauritian population began in the late 1830s with the immigration of indentured labourers to work on the sugar estates after the African slaves had been liberated. By 1860 they already made up two-thirds of the population and they have maintained this proportion ever since.

The Indo-Mauritians are unequally divided between Hindus and Muslims. In 1972 the population figures were 437,000 Hindus and 137,000 Muslims. In the nineteenth century most Muslims, who were predominately Gujaratis, had come to Mauritius as traders; wholesale and retail. They dominated the rice and cloth trades especially. The Hindus, who came from different areas, were predominantly recruited for work on the sugar estates, to replace the freed slaves and to meet the labour demands of an expanding industry. Many were misled about what awaited them in Mauritius. Once in Mauritius they had no choice but to take work as labourers on the sugar estates. The lucky ones obtained jobs as supervisors, or sirdars, and prospered. Even a few of the labourers somehow managed to improve their lot. In the last years of the nineteenth century, with the break up of some of the sugar estates, Indians managed to buy or rent small plots of land. By 1900 they owned about a quarter of the land growing sugar cane. By 1935 they owned 35 per cent of the land and a few had become owners of large estates.

Today the Hindus by and large still provide the labour force on the sugar estates but, as we shall see, an increasing number have tried to escape from their traditional role in the economy. As a community they were a relatively deprived group, educationally as well as politically, until the 1950s. Since then a rapid expansion of educational facilities has opened up new possibilities for the poorer members of the Indian community. Western-style education has opened the way to obtaining employment in government service and in the professions. Unfortunately the opportunities for

A Hindu temple at Triolet

employment fall far short of the numbers aspiring to such jobs. Indians with the necessary educational qualifications, however, are extremely unwilling to take work as labourers on the sugar estates.

The Creoles The Creoles make up the largest group of the population of Mauritius after the Indo-Mauritians. They form part of the 'General population' in the census along with the Franco-Mauritians and others of European descent. They constitute about 30 per cent of the island's population. They hold jobs in the Civil Service, some in the higher grades, in teaching and in the professions, including medicine and the law, and in managerial posts on the sugar plantations. Those with lower educational qualifications work as lower grade clerical workers and also as dockers and fishermen. Both women and men are employed in different kinds of domestic service.

Suggestions for revision

The plural character of Mauritian society has been one of its distinguishing features for the greater part of the island's history.

a) You should be able to identify the main groups in the country's society and their ethnic and other features, including their historical roles in the cultural, economic and political life of the island.

b) You should also be able to identify the influences within Mauritian society which help to give all Mauritians something in common and act as a counter-weight to those influences that divide society.

c) The term 'General population', which is used in the island's census returns, should also be understood.

Suggestions for further study

1 This chapter has treated a big and complex subject very generally. You may be interested, as a member of one of the groups which form a part of Mauritian society, to add to the information and the opinions contained in this chapter and to analyse in greater detail the distinguishing features of your own group. You may be able to learn much about your own group from older members of your family and community. They will remember how changes have come about in their own lifetimes in the island's social, economic and political life. In particular, perhaps, they will tell you how educational opportunities have changed for most of the island's children. Much recent history can be learned in this way from oral sources or by information passed down by word of mouth from one generation to the next. Since human memory is not very reliable, however, this sort of information needs to be checked in some other way before it can be accepted as accurate.

2 You might also like to think about what are called in this chapter the 'unifying forces' in Mauritian society. Are these, in your own experience, becoming more effective and more powerful in building up a truly Mauritian society?

CHAPTER 14

The people begin to stir: political developments 1922-1945

It is remarkable that the constitution of Mauritius remained unchanged between 1885, when Governor Pope Hennessy's constitution was introduced (see Chapter 11), and 1947, when Governor Mackenzie-Kennedy's constitutional proposals were accepted by the Colonial Office. In 1947 the constitution of Mauritius was the oldest in the British Empire.

The growth of political awareness

This did not mean that political activity amongst the people of Mauritius was completely dormant between 1885 and 1947. These years saw the prolonged arguments and party strife between the 'oligarchs' (the Parti de l'Ordre) and the 'democrats' (L'Action Libérale); and the brief visit of Mahatma Gandhi followed by the efforts of Manilal Doctor over a period of five years to stir the Indian community into political life (see Chapter 11). They also saw the emergence of the Labour Party and of a trade union movement; and it was these which mainly brought about the first changes in the constitution for over sixty years.

During this long period political and economic power remained firmly in the hands of a small group of people. In 1947 out of a population of about 450,000 there were still fewer than 12,000 people with the right to vote. Most of the electors were of European descent, Franco-Mauritians or 'Francos', but there were also a small number of non-Europeans, mainly urban, middle-class Creoles and Indians. The great mass of the Indian working classes, who made up 60 per cent of the population, had no effective political influence. From 1885 one of the nominated members of the Council of Government was usually an Indian, but he was chosen normally for his known moderate and conservative views. It is perhaps significant that when Dr X. Nallétamby, one of these nominated members, appeared before the Royal Commission of 1909, he admitted that his public position enabled him to know what was happening. In any case the Council was dominated by the official members and by its Franco-Mauritian majority. This group, the traditional ruling oligarchy, found little difficulty in persuading the governor and his officials to pursue policies aimed at the protection of their political and economic interests.

The government in London acquiesced in this state of affairs and so there were disproportionately few Indians employed in the public service. A report drawn up in 1941 by Mr Ridley, an official of the Indian Government visiting the island, showed that fewer than one-fifth of the police and well under half of the teachers were Indians. Only one district magistrate and one assistant police superintendent were Indians. At the higher levels the British filled the leading posts in the Civil Service as well as those of Governor and Colonial Secretary. Most of the judges were British whilst the key posts of senior police officers and magistrates were almost all held by Franco-Mauritians and French Creoles.

As far back as 1877 Governor Phayre, one of the few British governors who sympathised with the Indians and understood them, had written that if the Indians had not been a long-suffering people their treatment and conditions, their lack of rights and privileges, would have caused serious disturbances. Such disturbances did not occur until 1937 to 1938 and again in 1943. They were the beginnings of the pressure which in the end forced the Franco-Mauritian oligarchy to give up its monopoly of power.

Discontent in the sugar industry

The labour disturbances that flared up in August 1937 should not have been unexpected. The sugar industry had enjoyed years of prosperity during the early 1920s, but then the price of sugar fell and during the world depression of the early 1930s the industry went through a bad time. Its plight was made more serious still by a cyclone in 1931. Governor Jackson (1930-1937) arranged loans to prop up the industry and before his term of office ended there were signs that a revival was under way.

However, the years of depression had helped to bring to a head widespread dissatisfaction with the political and economic life of the island. The situation was bad enough for one of the more liberal members of the Council, Philippe Raffray, to state in the Legislature that 'the labouring classes have been living on wages hardly sufficient to keep them and their families alive'. Their wages were about thirty to forty cents a day, lower than those in any other British colony. Another member of the Council, Dr Maurice Curé, whose political views were unusually left-wing for a member of that body, was conducting a campaign for political reform. He organised a petition to the new King, Edward VIII, who had a reputation for sympathising with the working classes. The petition was sent in August 1936. It asked that the right to vote should be extended to all literate males. The Secretary for the Colonies replied that if a request for such a change came from the Council of Government it would be considered. There was no hope that this would happen. Dr Curé then asked in the Council that a Labour Department should be set up to protect the interests of the workers. He was ignored.

The founding of the Labour Party

Dr Curé's main achievement, however, was his launching of the Labour Party or Parti Travailliste. He was its first president. The party soon had agents throughout the island and membership cost only twenty-five cents a month. The leaders held meetings amongst the workers to increase their political awareness and encourage them to fight for higher wages and improved conditions. These leaders included Emmanuel Anquetil and Guy Rozemont, both orators with a popular appeal and, like Curé himself, Creoles; also Dr Seewoosagur Ramgoolam, recently returned from Britain, Pandit Sahadeo, and Harryparsad Ramnarain

Emmanuel Anquetil

who were Indians. The economic, social and political grievances of the workers were all emphasised at Labour Party meetings and the party undoubtedly played an important part in precipitating the disturbances on the sugar estates which began at the end of July 1937.

Labour disturbances 1937–1938

Several incidents passed off without violence. Even when over 800 workers and small planters from the Brisée Verdière region began to march on Port Louis, the march ended peacefully when they were turned back by a detachment of troops. Tension continued to mount, however, and strikes broke out in several districts, notably in Moka and Flacq. The first violence and loss of life occurred on the Union Flacq estate. This was one of the few large estates owned by an Indian, R. Gujadhur. In 1926 he had been one of the first two Indians ever to be elected to the Council of Government. Ironically, in July 1932, he had made his own contribution to spreading discontent amongst sugar workers. He had addressed a campaign for higher wages. He told the workers that they were the worst paid in the British Empire and that they were as badly off as the first indentured labourers to come to Mauritius nearly one hundred years earlier. On 13 August 1937, Gujadhur's own workers took their employer's advice and put to the test the genuineness of his sympathy with their demands. Gujadhur's reaction was to arm his staff with rifles. The crowd threw stones and other missiles and shots were fired in panic. Four workers fell dead, two of them killed by shots in the back; six others were wounded.

The workers' cause had its first martyrs. The sympathy of the whole Indian community was aroused. Violence spread to other parts of the island. Another man was killed on the Savanne estate in the village of L'Escalier. On this occasion the police had been patient in the face of much provocation for some time, but eventually they fired on the crowd. The dead man was not a sugar worker but his funeral was attended by large numbers of workers, who turned it into a mass demonstration by plantation workers and the Labour Party.

Tension remained high for some time, but there was no further loss of life. The strike movement spread from the estates to the docks in Port Louis where most of the workers were Creoles, mainly of African extraction. The Acting Governor, Mr E.W. Evans, proclaimed a state of emergency. The attitude of the planters, represented collectively in the Chamber of Agriculture, did not help matters. By the end of September the wave of strikes seemed to have subsided and the government urged the employers to negotiate. The planters were in no mood to do so, claiming that the action of agitators amongst the workers made negotiation impossible. In the end the government told them firmly that if they continued to refuse to discuss wages with their workers, they would be forced to accept conciliation from above.

Dr Maurice Curé

Commission of enquiry

Soon after the troubles began Mr Evans had set up a commission of enquiry. It was made up of the Procurator General, C.A. Hooper, who acted as chairman, Mr Lionel Collet, Protector of Immigrants, Dr Edgar Laurent and Philippe Raffray, both members of the Council of Government, and the president of the Chamber of Agriculture. The Labour Party, through Dr Curé and the Indian leadership, protested against the membership of the committee on the grounds that it included no representative of the workers. However, the workers' case was ably presented by Dr Curé and others, including some of the workers themselves. Dr Curé made it clear that, in his opinion, one of the most important causes of the discontent was that the workers had no political representation. The workers who gave evidence before the commission surprised the members by the ability and skill with which they presented their case and by their understanding of the issues. The chairman of the commission assured them that they would not be victimised by their employers.

Report of the commission

The report of the commission was placed before the Council in April 1938. It was very critical of many aspects of the sugar industry. It stated that wages were too low and should be increased by at least 10 per cent. The small planters were exploited by the owners of the processing factories to which they were all compelled to sell their sugar cane. The report accepted that the workers' lack of political rights was a major grievance amongst them, but it did not recommend that the franchise should be extended. The report condemned as 'obsolete and not in keeping with modern conditions' the sections of the Penal Code which prescribed imprisonment as the punishment for strikers, for a man should be free to sell his labour for the highest price he could get. It recommended that trade unions should be recognised and that a Labour Department should be created and its head, the Director of Labour, should take the place of the Protector of Immigrants. In April 1938, Mr H.T.W. Oswell, who had held a similar post in Malaya, became head of the new department with the task of looking into all labour problems. He made a good start by visiting Indian labourers in their villages and holding informal meetings with them.

Recognition of trade unions

In May 1938 the Industrial Association Ordinance implemented the recommendation that trade unions should be recognised. Within a few months of the Ordinance, twenty-five trade unions had been officially registered in different parts of the island. Another effect of this measure was to make strikes legal, provided that the dispute had first been submitted to a conciliation board. At the beginning of 1939 a Labour Ordinance came into effect. It was widely welcomed by the workers, one of whose leaders claimed that it gave them a new moral dignity. One benefit it conferred on Indian workers was that two Hindu festivals, the *Shivaratri* and the *Dipawali*, were recognised as estate holidays. The establishment of a Minimum Wages Board in the same year completed the changes designed to improve the lot of the workers. It remained to be seen how effective these measures would prove to be in practice.

The governorship of Sir Bede Clifford

In the meantime a new governor had arrived at the end of 1937 during what proved to be a lull in the disturbances. This was Sir Bede Clifford. He had been chosen with some care to handle a critical and delicate situation. His background suggested that the British Government had looked around for a man likely to act firmly and decisively in an emergency. Clifford was also known for his interest in Indian culture; he had had contact with the family of Rabindranath Tagore and had written extensively on Indian art and culture.

He confronted the issue of widening the franchise in an interesting way. While he felt that the mass of the Mauritian people were not ready for an extension of the franchise, he was most concerned that the humble classes of society should have the opportunity to speak on the matters that concerned them most. As he said, 'our first duty is to educate them in the day to day management of their own affairs, before plunging them into controversial politics or asking them to master the intricacies of parliamentary government'.

In 1938 Clifford appointed Mr A.L. Osman and Mr S. Seerbookun to the Council, to represent the interests of the small planters and workers. He was most impressed by their contribution. 'The two representatives of the small planters whom I appointed this year to the Council are both secretaries of co-operative credit societies and have acquitted themselves with confidence and ability in Council, and have made some excellent speeches, full of sound suggestions.'

In a despatch to the British Secretary of State in 1939, Clifford argued forcibly that representatives to the Council should come from elections within the co-operative credit societies and other industrial associations. He proposed nine 'occupational' seats on the Council, to be held by members whose property did not exceed a fixed maximum value. This would ensure that the capitalist element was excluded.

It is interesting to note that Seerbookun was replaced after his death by Seewoosagur Ramgoolam who thus became one of the official spokesmen for the Indian community. In an article written at the time, Ramgoolam said of Sir Bede Clifford: 'All His Excellency's references to labour and his thoughts for the labouring masses bring us to think that at long last there rises a new hope for this community of Indians . . .'

By one of his early actions, which outraged the Franco-Mauritians, Sir Bede Clifford showed dramatically that he was not going to be a puppet of the planting interests. A few months after his arrival on the island, Lord Dufferin and Ava, the Under Secretary of State for the Colonies, visited Mauritius. The governor gave a garden party at Le Réduit to mark the occasion. Sir Bede Clifford broke with tradition in inviting many representatives of rural society along with the more orthodox guests on such occasions. Conservative opinion was scandalised by this flouting of convention.

Governor Sir Bede Hugh Clifford

Dock strike 1938

The governor was forced, however, to take a somewhat different line when a dock strike broke out in August 1938. This time the centre of the trouble was at the docks in Port Louis, not on the sugar estates as in the previous year. Indirectly, however, the sugar industry and the interests of the planters were seriously threatened. Strikes began amongst the Creoles who supplied the bulk of the dock labour force. The strikes were timed to coincide with the arrival of the sugar steamers at Port Louis and the beginning of the cane harvest. A bottleneck was quickly caused by the accumulation of sacks of sugar at the docks waiting to be loaded. The dockers laid themselves open to retaliation by failing to use the conciliation board. Faced with this situation and its disastrous implications for the economy of the island, immediate and determined action had to be taken.

In his autobiography, *Proconsul*, Sir Bede Clifford makes his view of the strike clear. He firmly believed that the workers had been incited by agitators, chief amongst whom were Emmanuel Anquetil, whom he called 'an eloquent stump orator', and Dr Maurice Curé. He was convinced that the aim of these two was to wreck the conciliation machinery because it threatened 'to put them out of business'. It was an unlikely story; but it was the governor's excuse for acting swiftly and ruthlessly to break the strike. Anquetil was arrested and, without being charged or tried, exiled to the island of Rodrigues. He was not allowed to return until four months later. Other leaders were restricted. Three hundred dockers were also arrested and Indian loaders from the factories were 'smuggled' into the dock area to load the sugar onto the ships. Nineteen labour leaders from the estates were charged with frightening workers into striking. Eventually estate workers and dockers returned to work without gaining any advantage. The governor was complimented by the Colonial Office for his prompt and firm action, which it believed had taught the unruly elements in Mauritius a salutary lesson. Creech Jones, the opposition spokesman for colonial affairs in the House of Commons, was horrified by the harsh and arbitrary character of these actions and urged that the government should recognise and respect the workers' rights to express their industrial and political views and air their grievances. But the governor's action stood, and on this occasion no protest was made on behalf of the workers by the Indian government.

The war years

The early years of the war which broke out in 1939 were quiet years in Mauritius. This was not the result of any significant improvement in the lot of the workers. On the contrary, the workers' rights and conditions had deteriorated, in spite of the measures taken in 1938 and 1939 to improve them. Wages had failed even to keep pace with the rise in the cost of living between 1938 and 1943. In 1940 Mr Ridley, the secretary to the Indian Agent General in South Africa, visited Mauritius to report on the condition of the Indian workers for the Indian government. His report on the sugar workers presented a gloomy picture of people who were still a depressed class. Even though nearly two-thirds of the property in Port Louis was owned by Indo-Mauritians only two of them had succeeded in gaining election to the municipal council. Most disappointing of all, the legislation of 1938 to 1939 seemed to have brought little, if any, benefit to Indian workers on the sugar estates. The unions formed after the Industrial Association Ordinance were rendered largely ineffective when the employers dismissed their officials. The Labour Department, set up to watch over the interests of the workers, seemed, on the whole, anxious to keep the workers quiet. It had tried to obtain redress for workers who had been victimised by employers (a number of estate managers were taken to court) but its efforts were unsuccessful.

The 1943 disturbances

The quiet years ended in September 1943 with wage demands, strikes, violence and some loss of life. Demands for increased wages were hardly surprising. On some estates, particularly those in the crowded northern districts of the island, wages had fallen below the rate fixed by the Minimum Wages Board in 1941. Strikes began on several estates. On Beau Séjour an attempt was made by Labour Department officials to end the troubles by calling up the workers' leaders for national service. The employers refused to negotiate. They clearly felt that they were in a strong position as they had managed to put out of business all but two of the unions formed after 1938. One of the survivors was the North and Central Rivière du Rempart Labourers' Industrial Association. Its leader was Harryparsad Ramnarain, who had been secretary of the Labour Party. The workers of Belle Vue Harel estate asked Ramnarain to represent them before the conciliation board set up by the Labour Department to look into their claims. They were not members of Ramnarain's union but they did not trust any other leader. Under pressure from the Labour Department, Ramnarain accepted, without consulting the workers, an offer just equal to the minimum rate. The workers turned it down. A police officer went to Belle Vue Harel intending to arrest the leaders or 'agitators'. The workers gave him and his men a hostile reception and pelted them with stones. The police opened fire. Three workers were killed and sixteen seriously wounded. Several weeks later the labourers returned to work.

[1]The brothers Basdeo and Sookdeo Bissoondoyal played a prominent role in the cultural, religious and political emancipation of the Hindus.

On the completion of his studies in India Basdeo Bissoondoyal returned to Mauritius in 1939 and brought back with him the message that India was awakening and was taking cognizance of its cultural heritage as well as of its right to be free. Gandhi epitomized that dual struggle and Basdeo Bissoondoyal, inspired by Gandhi, founded the Jan Andolan movement and brought about the cultural and religious renaissance of the Hindus.

He appealed for unity among Hindus in their common fight against cultural and political imperialism. He was imprisoned several times, but his fight was successful not only in making Hindus of diverse backgrounds aware and proud of their common cultural heritage but also of making the colonial government aware of the emergence of the Indo-Mauritians as a force to reckon with.

The climax was reached in 1943 when a huge crowd celebrated the Maha Jag in Port Louis in perfect order. The Labour Party owes a great deal to the pioneering work of the Jan Andolan movement in the granting of the 1948

1 *See K. Hazareesingh* Histoire des Indiens a l'ile Maurice p 207-208 *Paris 1973*

Constitution and ultimately of adult suffrage.

In 1947 Basdeo's younger brother, Sookdeo, took up the political struggle in favour of the downtrodden. He was a fiery orator and inspired the masses. In 1948, after being elected first member for the Grand Port – Savanne constituency he created a sensation by refusing to shake hands with the Governor, preferring to join hands in the Indian 'namasté' style claiming later that his gesture was spontaneous when he saw the Governor shaking hands with non-Europeans in a contemptuous way. He moved the formal motion in the Legislative Council extending state subsidy to non-Christian religious establishments.

In the House of Lords, a debate on the subject was introduced by Lord Faringdon, who pointed out that trade unions of the modern type could hardly be said to exist among the estate workers in Mauritius. Without them the workers lived in deplorable conditions in wretched housing, with hardly any access to education. The remedy, in Lord Faringdon's view, was to replace the inadequate 'industrial associations' by proper trade unions; to open up educational opportunities; and ultimately to introduce political reform so as to break the planters' monopoly of political power, which he regarded as the root of all the trouble in the Mauritius sugar industry.

In the House of Commons in London, Creech Jones made his usual protests. A Commission of Inquiry was set up. Its report was a damning document. The employers had refused to accept any responsibility for what had happened and denied that the workers had any real grievances; they claimed that the workers had been incited by outsiders. In effect, the report stated that the employers were still behaving like feudal overlords. The Mauritian government took the side of the employers.

The report ended on a pessimistic, almost despairing note: 'Laws may be passed, administrative machinery may be erected [these were references to the 1938 to 1939 developments], money may be spent and the situation may nevertheless remain unchanged. This is particularly true of Mauritius. The situation as it exists today is the end product of an historical process which should be reckoned in generations.'

The fact that the British government decided to publish this report in the middle of a war was a measure of the seriousness with which, at last, it viewed the situation in Mauritius. There were signs that the urgent need for change had finally been realised. The new Governor, Sir Donald Mackenzie-Kennedy, was soon at work drafting a new constitution to begin the long, slow process of political change from oligarchy to democracy.

Suggestions for revision

You should know:

a) the story of the rise of the Labour Party and its part in
   i) the disturbances of 1937 to 1938 and 1943,
   ii) the emergence of political consciousness amongst the working-class peoples of the island and
   iii) the fight for the extension of the franchise and for a new constitution;
b) how non-Europeans became involved in the political life of Mauritius before 1948;
c) about the importance of key events, such as the labour troubles in 1937 to 1938 and in 1943;
d) about the work and importance of political figures of the period, such as Emmanuel Anquetil, Basudeo Bissoondoyal, Sir Bede Clifford, Dr Maurice Curé, Dr Seewoosagur Ramgoolam and Guy Rozemont.

Suggestions for further work

1 Again, as suggested in the previous chapter, you will be able to learn a good deal about some of the events described in this chapter from your parents and grandparents, some of whom may have seen the exciting events of 1937 to 1938. Remember, their stories of what happened may not be entirely accurate, especially if they were involved on one side or the other of the issues in dispute.

2 Why did it take so long for the ordinary people to become actively involved in politics? Why did it begin to happen when it did? Were there parallels for this slow progress of the mass of the people to a share in political power e.g. in African countries? Did it have something to do with the fact that Mauritius was a colonial territory?

CHAPTER 15

From oligarchy and colonial status to democracy and independence

Dr Seewoosagur Ramgoolam: early political career

For nearly a decade before this process began, a new figure had been emerging on the political scene as a champion of the oppressed Indian community and a leading member of the Labour Party. This was Dr Seewoosagur Ramgoolam, who returned to Mauritius in 1935 after fourteen years in Britain where he had completed his training as a doctor. Whilst in Britain he had served a useful political apprenticeship. He became a member of the Fabian Society and was, for a time, the secretary of the London branch of the Indian National Congress. In 1931, at the time of the Round Table Conference, he had met Mahatma Gandhi, Rabindranath Tagore and Srinivasa Sastri. He had made the acquaintance of several socialist politicians, including George Lansbury and Arthur Creech Jones, who became the Labour Party's spokesman on colonial affairs and, unofficially, a representative of colonial peoples and their interests. Dr Ramgoolam's return to Mauritius coincided with preparations for the centenary celebrations of the beginning of Indian immigration. He contributed an article to the *Indian Centenary Book*, published to mark the occasion. In it he wrote of the need to end 'the social cruelties rampant in our society'.

He knew that this would take a long time and would mean a long hard struggle against powerful vested interests. He was realistic about the patient groundwork that would be needed to influence public opinion and make the Indian workers aware of their political rights and responsibilities. With the help of socialist friends he established a daily newspaper, *Advance*. On Sundays he regularly visited Indian workers in their villages and began their political education. Slowly he built up support amongst the workers and earned the respect of the authorities. He was elected a member of the Port Louis Municipal Council.

Not long after this, in November 1940, he was nominated by the governor, Sir Bede Clifford, to replace one of the two Indians on the Council of Government who represented the interests of small planters and workers. His appointment was a break with tradition, for no one with such radical views had previously been nominated to the Council. His appointment did not mean that he had been won over to the establishment. He made it clear at once that he wanted genuine social reform which would benefit the workers. In his first speech in the Council he demanded that workers should be given the right to form themselves into trade unions and to take strike action.

In 1942 Sir Bede Clifford was replaced as governor by Sir Donald Mackenzie-Kennedy. Increasingly Dr Ramgoolam found himself out of sympathy with the new governor's approach and policies. He decided that his only course was to join the opposition so that he would be free to campaign openly for such causes as the extension of the franchise to the workers. When Mackenzie-Kennedy put forward his first constitutional proposals in October 1946, they did not go far enough for socialist leaders in Mauritius, for the franchise qualifications would still have excluded the mass of the people and left power in the hands of the whites. B. Bissoondoyal organised demonstrations against the proposals in Port Louis.

One of the most effective of these took the form of boycotting for the first time the 'Last Races' in 1947. Race meetings in Port Louis were organised by the Turf Club, an exclusive club whose membership at that time was restricted to Franco-Mauritians. The workers obtained a special leave on that day to attend the races. However, this gave the Franco-Mauritians an opportunity to look down on the labourers and their way of life and the special

Dr Ramgoolam, who became Sir Seewoosagur Ramgoolam in June 1965

day was dubbed in Creole 'les courses Malbar' which carried a pejorative meaning. Bissoondoyal campaigned against attending the races on that day and his move met with complete success. As from that year that particular race meeting no longer enjoyed popular support and, perforce, the appellation was dropped.

Dr Ramgoolam, with the support of men like Emmanuel Anquetil and Renganaden Seeneevassen, continued to press for a wider extension of the right to vote. Their cause was helped by a number of developments. The Labour Party had come to power in Britain in the first post-war general election. The war itself had brought a revolution in public opinion all over the world on issues like colonialism, self-determination and human freedoms and rights. It was becoming increasingly difficult for colonial powers such as Britain to ignore the mounting demands for freedom from foreign domination coming from rising nationalist movements in Asia and Africa. Lastly but by no means least in its impact on Mauritius, India gained her independence in 1947.

It did not take long for Britain's post-war Labour Government, elected in 1945 and faced with these pressures, to reach a decision in principle to work towards the granting of self-government and independence to all Britain's colonial territories. Once taken, this decision was maintained as a fundamental strand in Britain's policy towards her colonial territories. Subsequent British governments in the 1950s and 1960s, whether Labour or Conservative, continued with its gradual implementation. Alongside the pressures from nationalist and independence movements it was a major factor in bringing about the decolonisation of all Britain's colonial territories between 1947 and the late 1960s. The only alternative to such a policy would have been to resist, by force, the nationalist movements which began to emerge and gain momentum everywhere soon after the end of the Second World War. This would have been contrary to Britain's commitment to democratic principles. Equally important, it would have been unacceptably costly both financially and in terms of human resources and lives.

Mauritius was a part of Britain's colonial empire. The pressures there from nationalist movements were small in comparison with those in other larger territories. Nevertheless Governor Mackenzie-Kennedy was under pressure both from Britain, from the outside world and from inside Mauritius to move beyond his 1946 proposals for constitutional reform. In a letter to Creech Jones, who was now himself Colonial Secretary in the Labour Government, he admitted that his earlier proposals would no longer be acceptable in the atmosphere of 1948. Nevertheless both the Governor and the Colonial Secretary believed that it was too soon to move to universal suffrage. A commission appointed to make new proposals recommended in 1947 that the vote should be extended to anyone able to read and write simple sentences in any language used in Mauritius. This went far beyond the previous suggestion that the vote should be restricted to those holding the Primary Leaving Certificate. Anyone who had served in the armed forces should also qualify for the vote.

The Mackenzie-Kennedy Constitution 1947

The new proposals were accepted by the Colonial Office and were the basis for the election held in 1948. This was a real landmark in the constitutional history of Mauritius. In the previous election held in 1936 there had been 11,427 registered voters. In 1948 the number had risen to 71,236. Nearly two-fifths of the adult population could now vote. For the first time in the island's history the electorate included a significant number of workers. The governor presided over a Legislative Council consisting of nineteen elected, twelve nominated and three official members. For the first time the elected members in the Council outnumbered the nominated and official members. The island was divided into five electoral districts. Six members represented Plaines Wilhems and Rivière Noire; four represented Port Louis; and three members represented each of the districts of Moka-Flacq, Grand Port-Savanne and Pamplemousses-Rivière du Rempart.

The election of 1948

In the election of 1948, twelve of those returned to the Legislative Council were members of the Labour Party and these included several Indo-Mauritians. The struggle for the effective transfer of power from the old oligarchy to new men had really begun. Dr Ramgoolam and his colleagues, amongst the new men, made it clear that this was only the beginning. They had new objectives for the immediate future; and within the next decade they achieved most of them. These included the introduction of universal suffrage; an increase in the number of elected members in the Legislative Council; and the establishment of the principle that ministers should be responsible to the elected council.

These achievements were made in the face of opposition from the conservative elements in the country, who organised themselves after the election and fought a strong rearguard action to try to retain their old position of privilege as long as possible. They made as much as they could of the alleged danger of 'communalism': that is the danger that politics and political parties would develop and operate round the sectional interests of the different communities that made up the multiracial society of Mauritius. There was, it was claimed, evidence that the voting in the 1948 election had followed a communal pattern in that eleven candidates had been elected largely on Hindu votes in rural districts, eight by Creoles and one by Europeans. It is, however, not surprising that, with the extension of the franchise, the different groups should vote for candidates who they felt would support their own interests; and indeed this was the traditional pattern of voting when power was in the hands of the Franco-Mauritians. After the election, Dr Ramgoolam and others who genuinely wanted to encourage national unity and play down communalism tried to broaden the base of the Labour Party by attracting support from the different communities, particularly the non-European community. The main opposition to further change after 1948 was led by Jules Koenig and his Franco-Mauritian party, the Ralliement Mauricien or Parti Mauricien. They raised the bogey of Hindu domination, and until the next election they still held political power in Mauritius because they had the support of the nominated and official members of the Council.

The election of 1953

The election of 1953 brought genuine democracy a step nearer. The Labour Party increased its share of the elected seats to fourteen; but this was not enough to give the party an overall majority. The conservatives were still supported by most of the nominated and official members. Soon after the election the Labour Party newspaper, *Advance*, complained bitterly that in exercising his right to choose the nominated members, the governor had flouted the electors' wishes. Instead of reflecting the preference the electors had shown for Labour candidates he had chosen men who would prolong the political domination of the Franco-Mauritians. Further change was needed before the voice of the people in elections could become really effective. Dr Ramgoolam and the Labour Party demanded three main types of change: firstly, universal suffrage; secondly, a further increase in the number of elected members in the Legislative Council; and thirdly, the introduction of ministerial responsibility.

In 1953 the Labour Party managed to persuade the Legislative Council to pass a resolution calling for an extension of the franchise. Talks followed in London and the outcome was the offer of a new constitution in February 1956. It was proposed that the number of elected members of the Council should be increased to twenty-five; that universal suffrage should be introduced and that seven of the twelve members of the Executive Council should be chosen from the legislature. However, the second proposal was linked with another which made it unacceptable to the Labour Party; this was that elections should be held under a system of proportional representation. The Labour Party objected to proportional representation because they feared that in a multi-racial society such as that in Mauritius it would encourage people to vote in their communal groups. They also feared that it could undermine the strength and unity of the party.

The emergence of new parties and the election of 1959

In the face of this opposition the proposal of proportional representation was dropped. The details of the electoral system were to be worked out by an electoral commission under the chairmanship of Trustram Eve. The commission reported in 1958 and recommended an increase in the number of elected members to forty. On this basis the 1959 election was held. Before the election a number of changes had taken place in the pattern of political parties in Mauritius. The main opposition party, the Ralliement Mauricien, had taken a new name: the Parti Mauricien Social Démocrate (PMSD). It had done this largely because it realised that, in order to have a future, it must attract more support from the non-white population, particularly from the Creoles.

The Muslims had formed the Muslim Committee of Action (MCA), the Comité d'Action Musulmane (CAM). Its leader, Sir Abdool Razack Mohamed, had represented Muslim opinion at the London constitutional talks in 1955. At the time he was a member of the Ralliement Mauricien. The MCA was formed in 1958 when the Muslims realised that they were merely being used by the Europeans as allies against the Labour Party.

A fourth party, the Independent Forward Bloc (IFB), was also founded in 1958. It stood for the energetic revival of Indian culture and the consequent rejection of political systems based on Western culture.

The leading part in the founding of the IFB was played by Sookdeo Bissoondoyal, brother of Basudeo Bissoondoyal who had influenced his political thinking. Sookdeo Bissoondoyal had turned from school teaching to politics in 1948. In the election of that year he was elected to the Legislative Council as one of the members for the constituency of Grand Port/Savanne and one of the group of twelve Labour Party members. He also served as a member of the Executive Committee, but from 1953 he became increasingly critical of the Labour Party, believing that it had swerved from its original objective, namely the promotion of the ordinary working people's interests, and had forgotten its socialist aims. In 1957 he called for a boycott of the visit of Princess Margaret to Mauritius as a protest against corruption in the administration. It was during one of several terms of imprisonment in 1957 that he decided to form the IFB. Although he did not always agree with the policies of the Labour Party, Sookdeo Bissoondoyal did not hesitate to ally with it to seek the independence of Mauritius.

In spite of the existence of these two parties which were bound to attract some of the Indian votes, the Labour Party's fortunes reached a peak in the 1959 election. Of the forty elected seats, the party gained twenty-four. The IFB won six seats, the MCA five. Jules Koenig's PMSD won only three seats; and the remaining two went to Independent candidates.

One of the three PMSD seats was won by Gaëtan Duval, a young lawyer with a flamboyant personality, who was later to lead the party in succession to Jules Koenig. As a result of its decisive victory in this election the Labour Party was in a strong position to press for an early realisation of its final objectives: self-government and independence.

The 1961 Constitutional Conference

A constitutional conference at which all the Mauritian political parties were represented was held in London in June 1961. It soon became obvious that there was a serious rift between the PMSD and all the other parties. The PMSD did not want independence; the other parties did. The PMSD favoured some form of integration or association with Britain. The difference of opinion was easily explained. The PMSD, as the party representing Creoles and the Franco-Mauritian minority, was afraid of independence and of the political dominance of Indo-Mauritians which they believed would follow. Its fears were similar to those expressed by parties representing minority groups in other colonial territories, especially in Africa. As the date of independence came nearer, such fears became more real.

The PMSD claimed that most Mauritians were not yet ready to assume the responsibility of running their own affairs. This again was an argument that had been heard, and continued to be heard, from settler groups in African territories like Kenya and Northern and Southern Rhodesia. The PMSD argued that, if independence was inevitable, it should come slowly and with adequate safeguards for the minority groups. In Mauritius, as in other colonial territories, the British showed sympathy with these arguments.

Two stages to Independence

The PMSD was outnumbered, however, by the Labour Party and its allies who favoured as quick a transition to self-government and independence as possible. The PMSD representatives withdrew from the conference before any decisions were reached. It was agreed that self-government should be reached in two stages. In the first stage, effected in 1962, Dr Ramgoolam took the title of Chief Minister. The governor was to seek his advice on all ministerial appointments and on the question of the duration and date of dissolution of the Legislative Assembly. Dr Ramgoolam decided

Mauritians demonstrate at the constitutional talks in London, 1965

to speed up the transition to the second stage by bringing forward the date of the election from 1964 to 1963.

The election of 1963

In this election the Labour Party suffered a check. They won only nineteen seats out of forty and thus lost their overall majority, but they remained easily the largest party. The PMSD made some recovery with eight seats. The IFB had seven seats, the MCA four and the Independents two. The PMSD had benefited from the attractive personality of Gaëtan Duval. He was a colourful figure who had entered the legislature at the previous election and was to succeed Koenig as leader of the party in 1966.

In consultation with the Colonial Office, Ramgoolam formed an all-party coalition government after the election. Both the British Government and Ramgoolam were anxious to reassure the electorate and all sections of the community that their interests would not be overlooked. The second stage of progress towards self-government could now be effected. In March 1964 Dr Ramgoolam became Premier and the Executive Council became a council of ministers responsible to the Legislature. The coalition ministry proved to be a fragile one. The difference of opinion between the PMSD on the one hand and the Labour Party and its allies on the other persisted.

Mr Anthony Greenwood, the Colonial Secretary, and Sir Seewoosagur Ramgoolam, Premier of Mauritius

Constitutional Conference of 1965

Once again in 1965 all parties were represented in constitutional talks in London with the Colonial Secretary. Labour and its allies pressed for early independence. The PMSD put forward a scheme for 'associated status' with Britain, under which certain matters, including defence, foreign affairs and some constitutional decisions would have been kept under British control. They also asked that no final decision should be taken on the future of Mauritius before a referendum was held.

At the Constitutional Conference in London the British negotiators seemed reluctant to agree to an early move towards independence and showed sympathy with, and a readiness to listen to, the proposals of the PMSD. The prospects of Mauritius being granted independence as the MLP wished seemed to be threatened. This British attitude, however, was probably adopted as a means of persuading Sir Seewoosagur and the MLP to agree to the transfer to Britain of the Chagos Islands, as the price of a British grant of independence. If this was the case, the strategy worked. The MLP agreed not to raise objections to the transfer of the Chagos group to Britain as part of the British Indian Ocean Territories and to the evacuation of their inhabitants to Mauritius.

Other considerations, however, certainly influenced the final outcome. Sir Seewoosagur's reputation for moderation and tolerance and his long-standing connections with old Labour politicians in Britain were crucial. He was prepared to offer guarantees to the minorities including the appointment of an ombudsman[1],

1 *Ombudsman: an official first employed in Scandinavian countries and more recently in some other European countries to act as an arbiter between an ordinary citizen and government in cases where a citizen feels himself to be a victim of some form of injustice or discrimination.*

as proposed by Sookdeo Bissoondoyal, who would not be a Mauritian. Finally, with some misgivings but no doubt with African precedents in mind, the decision was taken that independence should be granted, provided a further election showed a clear demand for independence from the Mauritian people. It was to be granted, however, under a new electoral system designed to ensure the adequate representation of all minority groups. The end of 1966 was suggested as a possible date for independence after a six-month period of self-government. The Colonial Secretary ruled out both the PMSD's suggestion of a referendum and of a form of association with Britain. This was partly on the grounds that both did not conform to current British constitutional practice. They were, of course, though this was not said, peculiarly French.

The new electoral system

The final advance to independence was delayed by difficulties in reaching agreement on the form of the new electoral system. The PMSD made the most of these disagreements. An electoral commission, the Barnwell Commission, arrived in Mauritius early in 1966. Its recommendations were complicated and were felt to be too favourable to the urban electorate. Ramgoolam feared that the system would produce splinter groups and make stable government difficult. John Stonehouse, the Under Secretary for the Colonies, arrived in Mauritius to resolve the crisis. In the end the following arrangements were made. Mauritius was divided into twenty constituencies, each represented by three members. The island of Rodrigues was to form a two-member constituency. Eight seats would not be contested in the initial voting. They would be held in reserve and allocated to the eight best losers from the four groups which were judged to be inadequately represented after the main election. The main purpose of this 'corrective machinery' was to ensure adequate representation for the minority groups.

The election of 1967

The 'independence' election was finally held under this complicated system in August 1967. It was to take place under the scrutiny of observers from the Commonwealth, who would pass judgement on its fairness. Three parties, Labour, the MCA and the IFB, fought the election as the 'Independence Party'. The PMSD, now led by Duval, campaigned on the platform of something less than complete independence. The central issue was, therefore, clear-cut and the electorate's decision was equally decisive. The 'Independence Party' won thirty-nine seats shared as follows: Labour twenty-four, MCA four and IFB eleven. They polled 54.8 per cent of the votes. The PMSD won twenty-three seats with 43 per cent of the votes. The Commonwealth observers reported that, with few reservations, they were satisfied that the elections had been conducted fairly and with a minimum of violence. The very small number of spoiled ballot papers seemed to show that the great majority of the electors had understood the complicated electoral system. The final stage of the exercise, the allocation of the eight reserved seats, awarded an equal share to the government and opposition parties.

Self-government and independence

At last the way lay open for a rapid advance to independence. Mauritius became self-governing on 12 August 1967, immediately after the election. At the first meeting of the new Legislative Assembly on 22 August 1967, Sir Seewoosagur Ramgoolam put down for debate the resolution 'That this Assembly requests Her Majesty's Government in the United Kingdom to take the necessary steps to give effect, as soon as practicable this year, to the desire of the people of Mauritius to accede to Independence within the Commonwealth of Nations and that Mauritius be admitted to membership of the Commonwealth on the attainment of Independence.'

The resolution was passed and the British Government fixed 12 March 1968 as Independence Day. During the debate Sir Seewoosagur spoke hopefully of the country's future:

> We are meeting today on an historic and solemn occasion. By our decision today, Sir, we shall put Mauritius on the path of her destiny. It is a day of joy for all patriotic men and women, for on this day we are taking the formal step which will confer on our

Independence celebrations 1968

people freedom and bring them into their heritage . . .

With Independence there will come among the people of this country a sense of regeneration and there will arise in the hearts of our fellow countrymen a fervour and a determination to go forward and build for themselves and for future generations a strong and happy Mauritius . . .

Let us resolve that in our determination to build a better future for ourselves and our children we shall all be inspired by the loftiest principles of patriotism and love for our island home.

We have striven for many years now to create a new sense of unity out of our rich diversity and in the words of the poet let it be said for the glory of those who are fortunate to live at this hour:

'Bliss was it in that dawn to be alive.'

Such sentiments are expected of political leaders on these occasions; but what really mattered was the extent to which the hopes and ideals were realised in the future. It is time to examine how Mauritius has fared since her 'day of destiny'.

Suggestions for revision

The main concern of this chapter is the story of the struggle for, and the main steps towards, independence in Mauritius. You should know:

a) the main stages and landmarks on the road to independence, such as the new Constitution of 1948, the Constitutional Conference of 1961, and the elections of 1948, 1953, 1959, 1963 and 1967;
b) the names of and the difference between, the main political parties that emerged during this period, for example, the Ralliement Maurician (later the PMSD), the MCA and the IFB;
c) the part played by, and the ideas of, leading politicians and officials such as Dr Seewoosagur Ramgoolam, Gaëtan Duval, Jules Koenig, Sir Donald Mackenzie-Kennedy and the Bissoondoyal brothers.

Suggestions for further work

1 Once again, it would be interesting to do some 'oral' research with the help of older people in your family or your friends' families. Try to talk to people who had different views about whether it was best for Mauritius to become independent as soon as possible after the election of 1967 or whether it would have been better to have a longer period of self-government, as a preparation for complete independence.
2 Make sure you know the meaning of the following words: franchise (page 86), suffrage (page 88), proportional representation (page 89) and coalition (page 91).

CHAPTER 16

The economic and social history of Mauritius since the Second World War: economic problems and policies

The main features of the economy and society of Mauritius and the problems which have faced the governments of the island since the end of the Second World War have remained fairly constant. They were analysed in 1960 and 1961 by two commissions. The first of these was led by Professor Titmuss and Dr Abel-Smith from the London School of Economics, and reported in *Social Policies and Population Growth in Mauritius*. Professor Meade from Cambridge University made a broader survey of the *Economic and Social Structure of Mauritius*. The Meade Report has served as a guide to politicians and administrators ever since it was published.

The Meade Report: problems identified

Although Mauritius is normally classed as a developing country and part of the Third World, Professor Meade made the point in his report that, in some respects, it is not typical of the Third World. 'In many ways', his report stated, 'Mauritius is not underdeveloped. Some of its services are far advanced but too many eggs are in one basket.' In 1977 the average per capita income of Mauritians was £300, well above that of the world's poorest countries. Average incomes, of course, hide extremes of poverty and of affluence and Mauritius has its share of both. However, poverty in Mauritius is on a small scale compared with that found in the world's poorest countries.

The island's main problems were an economy dependent to a dangerous and unacceptable degree on a single crop, sugar; the dangers of an excessive rise in population; a high unemployment rate; and, since the mid-1970s, a serious balance of payments problem (i.e. an excess of imports over exports). The solutions, easy to prescribe but difficult to implement, were and remain: diversification of the economy; measures to control the growth of population, to encourage exports and to create new jobs. These are all linked to the need to educate the people of Mauritius to be aware of the problems and the corresponding solutions. They are also interlinked. Finally political stability is inextricably linked to the ability of politicians and governments to achieve some success in the control of these problems.

The Titmuss Report

The Titmuss Report forecast the disastrous consequences which would follow for Mauritius if the rate of population growth continued unchecked. Partly as a result of the remarkable success of the government's campaign against malaria since the Second World War, the death rate declined dramatically in the 1960s. The birth rate, on the other hand, remained high. A steady improvement in medical care had increased life expectancy. The population was increasing at the rate of 3 per cent per year. By the year 2000 this would have brought the population of Mauritius close to 3 million.

Population problems

In the particular case of Mauritius, Professor Titmuss and Dr Smith were on safe ground in identifying an unchecked population growth as a threat to the future prosperity and development of the island. The physical area of the island is so small that its capacity for supporting more people is limited. It is worth remembering, however, that in the world in general there is not necessarily any direct link between poverty and a high population density.

The idea that population growth in itself is always a bad thing, that it is bound to lead to a fall in living standards, to food shortages, to higher unemployment and, in general, to greater poverty, is no longer accepted by experts. One has not got to look far to realise that under-population is at least as likely to lead to social and economic problems. Most African countries, for example, are under- rather than over-populated. If many people in Africa are poor and underfed it is not because there are too many of them. The fault lies in the economy and in its management. The problem of unemployment is solved by creation of more jobs through expansion of the economy, not by slowing down population growth and reducing population.

Solutions to the problem

Having warned against the possibility of economic and social disaster the Titmuss Report went on to make recommendations for avoiding it. Mauritius had much on its side. From the point of view of easy communications, its smallness was an advantage. Educationally it was ahead of most Third World countries. So long as population was kept within reasonable bounds it could become one of the prosperous, not one of the poor, areas of high population density. Quite simply, families were too large and the birth rate was too high. Family planning, later marriages and the ideal of a three-child family were the main ways to restrict population growth.

Family planning

In an island with a multi-racial, multi-religious population, family planning could be a delicate policy for the government to pursue. The large Roman Catholic element in the population rejects, through the teaching of its church, the use of contraceptives. The Muslim community, a minority group, is reluctant to restrict its growth rate. The first offical government support was given to the Mauritius Family Planning Association (FPA) in 1968, ten years after its foundation. Since independence the Association's efforts have been assisted by those of the Action Familiale, a Catholic organisation giving advice on birth control methods acceptable to the Roman Catholic Church. More than half of the clinics run by the FPA were brought under the Ministry of Health in November 1972. A separate division of the Ministry is concerned with maternal and child health and family planning. The programme became part of the First National Development Plan.

The whole campaign to control population growth has had remarkable success. The rate of growth was down to about 1.7 per cent in 1975, a decline rarely achieved even in the developing world. It seemed that it might fall to something approaching 1 per cent during the 1980s. Unfortunately the campaign seemed to lose its momentum in the late 1970s and, although the disastrous rise in population which Titmuss warned the country against has been avoided, population growth remains a potential danger to the future prosperity of Mauritius.

Emigration

The only other possible way of checking population growth is through a policy of encouraging emigration. The Mauritian government has used this method also. In the 1960s, the emigrants were mainly Creoles, motivated often by a desire to escape the danger of Hindu domination. They went mainly to Australia (just over 40 per cent), Britain (just under 40 per cent) and, to a lesser extent, to France and South Africa (about 4.5 per cent in each case). In the 1970s an increasing number of Indo-Mauritians joined the emigrants. Almost all went to Britain where they worked mainly in hospitals. There were many Mauritians working as male nurses in British mental health hospitals. Emigration, however, can have no more than a marginal effect on population. In the whole of the 1960s, fewer than 17,000 people left the country.

Unemployment

Some of those who emigrated left to find suitable employment and emigration, therefore, made a contribution to the solution of another problem, that of unemployment. Again, however, the contribution was a small one and the problem an increasingly serious one. An attempt to understand the high level of unemployment shows how many of the country's problems are interlinked. The dominant place of sugar in the economy, a problem in itself, does not help. At first sight this may seem a strange claim to make. After all the sugar industry is still the largest employer of labour in Mauritius. It provides jobs for 60,000 workers, about one-third of the work force. However, employment in the industry is seasonal. Many of the jobs are only available during the harvesting season from August to December. Many of those employed at this time may become unemployed during the rest of the year. Another reason for claiming that the sugar industry indirectly increases unemployment lies in the growing reluctance of educated young men to work in the cane fields. The government's success in expanding educational opportunities has also helped to create this situation. Some young men who have succeeded in gaining a Cambridge School Certificate or some other educational qualification would rather remain unemployed than undertake manual labour in the sugar industry. Another feature of education in Mauritius further complicates the issue. Too high a proportion of young Mauritians have had an 'academic' education; too few have had a technical or practical training.

Economic planning

Economic planning in Mauritius goes back to the year 1957, when the government's Economic Planning Committee drew up a *Plan for Mauritius*, a five-year programme of government projects. This had to be abandoned in 1960 when the destruction caused by the cyclones 'Alix' and 'Carol' faced the government with much more urgent problems in its 1960 to 1965 Reconstruction and Development Programme. The reports of Titmuss and Meade also helped to point the way to economic and social priorities and an Economic Planning Unit was set up. After independence the Unit became part of the Ministry of Economic Planning and Development which drew up the First National Plan, a four-year plan, from 1971 to 1975.

The First National Plan 1971-1975

In drawing up this programme the planners recognised the three major problems: the mono-crop economy (sugar), the rate of population growth and unemployment. Its main objective was to create employment. It aimed at creating 52,000 new jobs in the first four years. It slightly exceeded its target in this respect as well as in the economic growth rate achieved; 10 per cent instead of 7 per cent.

The Mauritius Economic Review, published by the Ministry of Economic Planning and Development in 1976, summed up the achievements of the 1971 to 1975 plan with justifiable satisfaction:

> The 1971-1975 Plan therefore sets out as its main objectives the creation of productive employment, steady and viable economic growth and more equitable distribution of income.
>
> The 1971-1975 Plan period was undisputably one of solid economic achievements and all round progress. The targets laid down in the Plan in respect of employment and income were surpassed. Investment in the basic social and economic infrastructure of the country took place at an accelerating rate. Impressive results were also achieved in the diversification of the economy away from the monocropping of sugar. Positive results were also obtained in the efforts made to reduce the rate of population growth.

A textile factory in the Export Processing Zone scheme

Export Processing Zone

The success of the job creation programme was achieved largely through industrial development, much of it under the Export Processing Zone project and some as a result of the government's own action programme carried out by the newly created Development Works Corporation under the name of 'Travail pour tous'.

The first Export Processing Zone, set up in the Port Louis area, was, as its name indicates, an area where industrial enterprises were set up for the purpose of producing goods for export. Export Processing Zones were first created in the Far East, and now exist in other parts of south-east and south Asia. Export Processing Zones offer advantages and opportunities both to foreign investors, including multi-national corporations, to domestic investors and to the people of the countries in which they are based. To the investors they offer above all a plentiful supply of cheap labour, mostly provided by girls and young women. For the host countries they create opportunities for employment through the establishment of manufacturing industries. In Mauritius they are an attempt to contribute to the solution of the island's economic and social problems by creating new jobs, diversifying the economy and stimulating exports. Various incentives and concessions were available to encourage foreign investors as well as Mauritians to invest capital in these enterprises. Facilities for cheap transport, power and water were provided; certain tax exemptions were offered as well as duty-free import of machinery, raw materials and other necessary items. By 1975 the Export Processing Zone scheme had provided nearly 10,000 new jobs and by the following year eighty firms were operating under the scheme, many financed and controlled from abroad. French, Hong Kong, Indian and German firms were prominent. The project was continued in the Second Development Programme, 1975 to 1980, and jobs provided totalled nearly 20,000.

By far the most successful sector of manufacturing industry within the scheme has been textiles. Nearly fifty firms are involved in this area but Mauritius has serious competition to face in the field, notably from Hong Kong with a much larger tradition in the industry and over 1000 firms producing vast quantities of goods. The Mauritian government needs to strike a delicate balance between allowing the firms to produce their products at a low cost, and satisfying the aspirations of the Mauritian labour force. The 'Travail pour tous' programme provided jobs for 5000 to 6000 people in public works including the building of roads, schools and classrooms, public buildings and forestry schemes. Between 1974 and 1975 the Development Works Corporation which administered the 'Travail pour tous' programme was also made responsible for a Rural Development Programme, aimed at raising living standards in some of the island's poorest villages.

Tourism

The expansion of tourism was another major success of the 1971 to 1975 programme. Between 1970 and 1974 numbers of tourists almost trebled (from 25,000 to 73,000), earnings from the industry more than quadrupled (Rs 27 million to Rs 112 million) and workers directly employed trebled (1500 to 4500).

The Second National Plan 1976-1980

The *Economic Review* of the period 1971 to 1975 ended on an optimistic note both on the progress achieved and on future prospects:

> To sum up, the significant achievements of the economy during the plan period 1971-1975 were reflected in GNP growth, the expansion of the manufacturing section including the export processing zone and the dent made into the unemployment problem. These clearly bear out the success of the development policy followed by the country and indicate that the base for more rapid development in the future has been firmly established.

Unfortunately the prediction in the last sentence was not fulfilled. The Second National Plan, 1976 to 1980, did not have the success of the first. The target, for example, of 76,000 new jobs was not achieved: the continued growth of industry in the Export Processing Zone did not take place. Many factors contributed to this failure to maintain the economic momentum of the early 1970s. The high level of government spending in the 'Travail pour tous' programme placed a heavy strain on the economy.

The sugar industry runs into trouble

The sugar industry, after enjoying a boom which reached a peak in 1974, suffered from falling prices. Without the agreement with the EEC under the Lomé Convention (see page 100), the effect of this trend would have been more serious. As a result of this, and the rise in oil prices after 1973, the balance of trade tilted heavily against Mauritius. Imports, stimulated partly by rising wages, almost doubled between 1974 and 1978. The value of exports fell because of the slump in the sugar industry. From a slight surplus in 1974, the country's trade fell into a deficit of over Rs 500 million in 1976, and over Rs 1000 million in 1978. The sugar industry's troubles were made worse by a substantial rise in wages and prices and by the strike of dock workers in Port Louis in August 1978. Perhaps some good for the industry has resulted from these developments. High wages have at last forced the industry, with government approval, to turn to greater mechanisation and to make maximum use of all parts of the crop in producing a wide range of by-products. Cane waste, for example, is used as fuel for sugar factories, for the making of board for use in the furniture industry and for the production of alcohol to be used as an alternative to petrol.

Diversification in agriculture

The sugar industry also played a leading part in the struggle to diversify the agricultural sector of the economy. Revenue made by the industry was used to promote the growth of other crops. Of these, tea is the most important and is the country's next most important agricultural export after sugar. Tea bushes with their deep roots are able to withstand the destructive power of cyclones better than most crops. A Tea Control Board established in 1959 controls the cultivation and sale of the crop and also its quantity and quality. Other export crops grown in significant quantities include tobacco and also fibre.

A modern sugar refinery in Mauritius

A wide range of vegetables is cultivated, many of them inter-cropped between the rows of sugar cane, in an effort to increase the proportion of food produced on the island. The need to import large quantities of food, particularly rice, is one of the main reasons for the unfavourable balance of trade. About 30 per cent of the cost of imports is for food and half of this is for rice and wheat, both of which are subsidised. A National Food Production Committee was set up in 1974. Its task was to make recommendations for the 'most practical and efficient means of rapidly increasing local food production'. Considerable progress has been made towards the achievement of self-sufficiency in vegetables. The staple crops of rice and wheat are never likely to be grown in quantities that will significantly reduce the import bill, but experiments in the growing of rice are being continued, with the help of Chinese advisers.

Efforts were also made to produce maize, meat and dairy produce. The main success in this field was with poultry and by the end of the 1970s production reached 65,000 frozen chickens a week, sufficient for the island's needs. In Mauritius chicken is eaten by all the different communities. The fishing industry has made disappointing progress. Too many foreign fishermen with up-to-date ships and equipment have recently begun to exploit the waters of the Indian Ocean. Fishing fleets from Japan, Taiwan and South Korea are based in Mauritius.

Attempts to diversify the Mauritian economy have thus achieved some success. Nevertheless there is no escaping the fact that the prosperity of Mauritius remains overwhelmingly dependent on its sugar crop. The simple truth is that few crops are able to withstand the cyclones as well as sugar and few seem to flourish as well in the peculiar and difficult agricultural conditions of the island's rock-strewn landscape. Sugar still covers 90 per cent of the cultivated land; employs nearly 60,000 people, one-third of the total employed population; and, along with its main by-products like molasses, accounts for almost 70 per cent of the value of the country's exports. As shown above, however, the extent of sugar's dominance has declined in recent years. Amongst the reasons for this have been the slump in sugar prices and the rise in labour costs since the boom year of 1974. Mechanisation has increased but there is a limit to the part machines can play in harvesting the crop in the difficult rocky cane fields. There is also a reluctance to carry mechanisation too far in a country where the creation of more jobs is still a priority of government policy. One result of these developments was that the production target set for sugar of 800,000 tonnes by 1980 in the Second National Plan had to be abandoned. Early in 1980 the price of sugar in the world market began to rise again because, for the first time in six years, world production fell short of consumption. One good result of the difficult years between 1974 and 1980 was the remarkable skill and ingenuity which enabled every part of the crop to be turned to some use and profit.

Special agreements for the sugar industry

Finally it should be made clear that Mauritius and other sugar-producing areas have been protected from the worst effects of low prices on the open market by the guaranteed market for sugar at guaranteed prices in the EEC. The lesson of the last six years is to underline the wisdom of the Prime Minister and his colleagues who negotiated the terms of the Lomé Convention with the EEC countries. The story behind the Lomé Convention and its special sugar protocol must be understood.

The Commonwealth Sugar Agreement 1951

In 1951 Britain made a Commonwealth Sugar Agreement with the sugar-producing members of the Commonwealth. Under this agreement Mauritius sold around 60 per cent of her sugar crop to Britain. This arrangement was the pivot of the Mauritian economy and her main source of revenue from exports. On 1 January 1973, Britain became a member of the European Economic Community (EEC) or European Common Market. As a member of the EEC she had to abandon, within five years, all her existing trade agreements with other countries. These included the Commonwealth Sugar Agreement which was due to expire at the end of 1974. Britain made it known that she intended to continue to give her Commonwealth partners access to Britain for their sugar

Cutting jute

and this commitment was written into her treaty of accession to the EEC.

The Lomé Convention 1975

During 1974 Britain's negotiations ran into difficulties with her EEC partners but eventually, in a special sugar protocol which became part of the Lomé Convention signed in 1975, satisfactory terms were agreed.

The Lomé Convention was a new agreement signed between the extended European Community[1] and forty-six developing countries from Africa, the Caribbean and the Pacific, the ACP countries. They included all of Britain's Commonwealth partners previously in the Commonwealth Sugar Agreement. The Lomé Convention replaced the earlier Yaoundé Convention. This had admitted the old African colonies of France and Belgium as associate members of the EEC, with certain trading privileges. Mauritius, because of her old ties with France, had become a member of the Yaoundé Convention in May 1973. She was the first Commonwealth country to become an associate of the EEC before Lomé. Mauritius thus had a special role in the negotiations which led to the conclusion of the sugar protocol. The thirteen ACP sugar-producing countries were guaranteed a market for 1.4 million tons of sugar a year at prices linked to the prices paid within the EEC to producers of beet sugar. Of this quota, the share of Mauritius was 500,000 tons, the largest of any single country by a big margin. Fiji was next with 163,000 tons. The price of sugar on the open market happened to be much higher than the EEC price at the time and Britain was permitted to pay a special price (£260 per ton) for her share of ACP sugar, a compromise between the EEC price of £157 per ton and the world price of just over £300. Mauritius believed that she had obtained a good deal and falling world sugar prices over the following five years proved her to be right. The Lomé Convention also gave free access to the EEC for all manufactured products of the member states. This was of value to Mauritius as the factories of her Export Processing Zone began to produce goods for export. The Lomé Convention was important above all, however, because it provided satisfactory new terms for the marketing of Mauritian sugar after the expiry of the Commonwealth Sugar Agreement in 1974.

Suggestions for revision

a) It is important to understand the main economic and social problems that faced Mauritius both before and after independence.
b) You should also know what steps were taken by the government of Mauritius to try to solve these problems and how successful their policies have been.

Suggestions for further work

1 Make a list of the reasons why, in spite of all the efforts made to diversify the economy, sugar has continued to dominate it.
2 Find out about other economies which, like that of Mauritius, are largely dependent on one crop or one commodity. Why are most, if not all, of these in the 'Third World' or less developed world? They are also usually countries which, until recently, were colonial territories.
3 What is meant by a 'balance of payments' problem? Why has Mauritius had such a problem since about 1975?

1 *Initially (1958) the EEC had six member states: France, West Germany, Italy, Belgium, Holland and Luxembourg. Three new members, Britain, Denmark and Eire, were admitted in 1973, extending the membership to nine.*

CHAPTER 17

Social problems and policies since the Second World War

The overall picture of the recent achievements of Mauritius in the economic and social field would be incomplete without reference to the very considerable progress made in four main areas of social policy: pensions, housing, health and education. It is here that the socialist aims of government since independence can most clearly be seen.

Pensions

The foundation of a National Pension Scheme was laid in 1957 with the introduction of a non-contributary Old Age Pensions Scheme for all over sixty-five. The qualifying age was later lowered to sixty. A much more comprehensive National Pension Scheme was drawn up in 1975 by the Ministry of Social Security. It covered the old, the maimed, the infirm and widows and orphans against the worst effects of need and want. All are entitled to the basic benefits. A contributory section provides benefits additional to the basic provisions and a further section provides benefits for those suffering industrial injury.

Housing

Mauritius has a long history of ramshackle, squalid housing for the mass of its working people which has lasted into recent times. Box-like, make-shift shacks are still to be found. The damage caused by periodic cyclones does not make the housing problem any easier to solve. The first serious efforts to improve housing on a large scale were probably sparked off by the widespread havoc caused by the two devastating cyclones, 'Alix' and 'Carol', in 1960. About 25,000 slum houses were destroyed. It was a good time to tackle the housing problem with vigour. The Central Housing Authority was set up and launched a programme for the re-housing of those made homeless by the cyclones. Thirteen thousand houses were built by 1970 for purchase over twenty-five years by monthly payment. The houses were built all over the island in both urban and rural areas. In 1970 purchase on easier terms was introduced for the poorest tenants.

The Mauritius Economic Review of the First National Plan, 1971 to 1975, admitted that the lower income groups' efforts to obtain better housing 'were seriously hampered by the sudden increase in the price of land and cost of construction'. Cyclone 'Gervaise' in February 1975 further aggravated the problem. No less than 13,000 victims of the cyclone reported that their houses had been completely destroyed or damaged beyond repair. An emergency programme for the construction of 7600 houses was planned. Seven thousand of these were to be built by the Central Housing Authority and the remaining six hundred by the Sugar Industry Labour Welfare Fund. The Prime Minister's special Cyclone 'Gervaise' Reconstruction Fund was set up to finance the rehousing of destitute widows and old people of over sixty years.

Another agency, the Mauritius Housing Corporation, was created in 1963 to provide mortgage loans for middle-class people who wanted to own houses. As house construction costs rose, the Corporation began to build blocks of flats of which Harbour View Scheme in Port Louis was the first example. Other

Ribbon development housing

blocks of apartments were later built in several other places. The Corporation has also been involved in financing the reconstruction or repair of houses for 'Gervaise' victims and in the general attempt to raise building standards by planning 'model' houses. In the last twenty years much has been done to raise standards and improve the construction of houses and to ensure that they are provided with basic facilities for water, sanitation and lighting.

Health

Standards of health and medical care for the majority of Mauritians were low before the 1940s. If some of the infectious diseases which had caused the worst epidemics in the eighteenth and nineteenth centuries had been virtually eradicated since 1920, two serious scourges still remained; malaria and tuberculosis. The first great step to improved health and a lower death rate came as a result of the success of the campaign in the 1950s against malaria. In 1973 the World Health Organisation gave Mauritius a certificate of malaria eradication.

A year before independence, in 1967, Mauritius had eight hospitals. Two of these were large ones: the Civil Hospital in Port Louis and the Candos at Quatre Bornes. There were six smaller ones in Mahébourg, Flacq, Souillac, Moka, Montagne Longue and Poudre d'Or. Ten years later there were eleven hospitals and these included the new one, the Sir Seewoosagur Ramgoolam National Hospital, which was completed in 1972 and since then has been the country's main hospital. During the First National Plan the existing hospitals had been improved and some of them had become specialist hospitals: Montagne Longue in psychiatry, Poudre d'Or in tuberculosis, Moka as an opthalmic centre.

The medical service is well staffed with doctors and nurses and other personnel, including midwives and radiographers. Nurses are trained mostly at the Mauritian School of Nursing at the Sir Seewoosagur Ramgoolam National Hospital.

Education

In its education services also Mauritius has reached a stage of development in advance of most developing countries. The majority of people, both children and their parents, are hungry for education, believing it to provide the means of economic and social advancement. Strangely enough, this attitude towards education encourages the existence of a large proportion of rather poor schools. Education is valued not for its own sake, but as a means to an end. Until after the Second World War, opportunities for education were restricted to the wealthier sections of the population: the Europeans and a small number of Indians, Creoles and Chinese. Formal education was provided, for the most part, in privately run schools, though from 1941 the Ministry of Education became responsible for the few state and state-aided schools. Most of the people had no formal education and were illiterate.

The new constitution of 1947 and the extension of the franchise made it imperative to extend educational facilities. Resources were limited, however, and a basic decision had to be taken on the use of these resources. Priority was given to the expansion of primary education between the ages of five and twelve and this remained the main educational objective until the mid-1970s. By this date primary education was free, but still not compulsory. Nearly 90 per cent of the primary age group were attending school. In the meantime, increased provision was being made for education at other levels. In a multiracial society, language presented a problem in education. The Ward Report on Education in the early 1940s recommended that English should be the language of instruction in schools. In fact, much teaching at a young age is carried out in Creole, the language understood by the vast majority of the people, whatever their ethnic origin. English and French are compulsory languages and provision is now made for the teaching of a number of Indian languages, Hindi, Urdu, Tamil, Telugu and Marathi, as optional subjects, along with Arabic and Mandarin.

The First National Plan

When the First National Plan was begun in 1971, shortage of school accommodation was a major obstacle to further progress in education at all levels. A shift system, for example, had to be operated in primary schools so that a maximum number of children could be given some schooling. The Plan set out its main objectives in education as provision of free primary school education for all children; expansion of the facilities for secondary education and vocational education and training; and provision for the teaching of technical subjects and integrated sciences as well as academic subjects. The Plan also aimed to offer equality of educational opportunity to all, according to their educational potential.

Primary and Secondary Education

An ambitious programme of primary school building was launched after independence to give full-time education to all children of primary school going age. This programme has had considerable success.

At secondary level there were many schools not worth the name and housed in very inappropriate buildings. The Government, with the assistance of the World Bank, constructed 12 new Junior Secondary Schools, which have now become secondary schools offering a full five-year course up to the School Certificate; and, with the assistance of the European Development Fund, a Form VI College and two secondary schools teaching up to Form VI.

Tertiary Education

The University of Mauritius was opened in 1965 but did not function very effectively before independence. Since then it has evolved along lines particularly suited to the special needs of a developing country. It runs courses and carries out research in agriculture, technology and administration.

The Mahatma Gandhi Institute was opened in 1972 with assistance from the Indian Government primarily to encourage the study of Indian languages and culture. It has a secondary school attached to it. In 1976 a School of Mauritian, African and Asian Studies was established within the Institute for the study of the history and culture of the island with particular reference to the two continents with which so many of its peoples have connections.

In 1974 the Mauritius Institute of Education was set up as a UNDP/UNESCO project to train secondary school teachers and carry out curriculum development. It was largely successful in these two areas, and with the integration of the Mauritius College of Education (ex-

A primary school at Floréal

Teacher's Training College) within it, it is now also training primary school teachers and carrying out curriculum development at the primary level.

Mention should also be made of the setting up of the Mauritius College of the Air, which was intended to supplement formal and to promote non-formal education.

Vocational training

Some vocational training centres were opened to cater for artisanal orientation, and two Industrial Trade Training Centres for lower level technical training. A more recent development has been the setting up, with assistance from the French Government, of an ambitious 'Lycee Polytechnique' to provide higher level technical training.

UNESCO Report on Education in Mauritius
In spite of these provisions for technical and vocational education and training, a UNESCO Report on Education in Mauritius in 1974 was critical of the island's education system, partly on the grounds that there was not enough of this kind of education. The report mentioned a 'lack of clearly defined objectives and planning expressed in terms of the country's needs'. It also mentioned the need for improvement and change in curriculum content, in examinations, in methods of teaching and teacher training and in supervision of the system. An Institute of Education established in 1973 became involved in improving the system, although in a field as controversial as education, there was bound to be much debate about how improvement and change were to be brought about. One of the Institute's main tasks was to train teachers for secondary schools, though it will also train some primary teachers. A teachers' training college already existed for training primary teachers and after 1972 its students followed a two-year course divided into four-monthly periods spent alternately in college and in school.

It is difficult not to acknowledge that the brief story of the economic and social life of Mauritius presented in the last two chapters is one of steady progress and achievement in the face of difficult problems. In particular, since independence the Ramgoolam governments have grappled with problems common in the developing world with more success than most. This very success, however, has sometimes created new problems. Widespread education has produced many educated young Mauritians who have often been unable to find the kind of employment they want. They are dissatisfied. Rising living standards have led to more imports which have created an adverse balance of trade. Economic and social progress has been made; but problems, sometimes new and more complex ones, still remain. Political stability is very difficult to achieve in such conditions. It is time to turn to the political story of Mauritius since independence.

Suggestions for revision

a) You should know what improvements have been made in the social services (housing, health and education) of Mauritius since 1945 and since independence in particular. It is not enough to know simply that more houses, more schools or more hospitals were built; you should know what kind of schools they were (primary, secondary or technical and vocational), whether hospitals were general or specialist hospitals and whether the services were free and available for all.

Suggestions for further work

1 Distinguish between the following:
   i) the Central Housing Authority
   ii) the Mauritius Housing Corporation
   iii) the Sugar Industry Labour Welfare Fund.

   What contribution did each of these make to the provision of new housing in Mauritius?

2 On a map of Mauritius, mark the location of the country's hospitals
   a) in 1967, b) in 1977 and c) today.
   Underline the places which have specialist hospitals and also name other types of institution which form part of the country's health service.

3 The number of pupils attending secondary schools in Mauritius doubled in the ten years following independence. When the rate of growth of an education system is as

The University of Mauritius at Le Réduit

high as this, it becomes difficult to maintain standards throughout the service. Make a list of the reasons for this.

4 What are the advantages and the disadvantages of providing education by radio through the College of the Air? Make a list of each.

5 What do the initials UNESCO stand for? Why was the education system of Mauritius criticised in 1974 by the UNESCO Report on Education in Mauritius?

The same criticism could be made of the education systems in many other countries of the Third World. Why have the education systems in these countries developed in a way which is now considered unsuited to the needs of developing countries? Is it the fault of:

i) the colonial powers that ruled these countries until recently;
ii) the governments that have ruled since independence;
iii) the people living in the countries;
iv) a combination of all these?

CHAPTER 18

Politics since independence

The need for coalition government

In the last two chapters (Chapters 15 and 16) a great deal has already been written about Mauritian politics since independence. Coping with economic and social problems constitutes a large part of the work of the politicians and government in any country. There is, however, one part of the story which has not been told and it is an important part in any democracy: the mechanics of achieving and holding political power. It is the story of elections and of the need, at times, for political parties and groups to from coalitions in order to exercise power effectively.

Since the election of 1963 this has been a necessary feature of the political life of Mauritius. The last time a single party won an absolute majority in a general election was in 1959. In the three elections held since then, those in 1963, 1967 and 1976, no party has won more than half the seats. No party, therefore, has been in a position to govern without the support of at least one other party or group. In the 'independence' election of 1967 the Independence Party won thirty-eight out of the sixty-two seats. The remaining twenty-three seats were won by the PMSD. The Independence Party, however, was not, in the true sense of the word, a single party. It was a fragile coalition made up of three separate parties, the Labour Party, the Muslim Committee of Action and the Independent Forward Bloc, which were united on the question of immediate independence but not necessarily on other issues.

The Labour PMSD Coalition 1969-1973

Within a year of independence this uneasy alliance between the Labour Party, the MCA and the IFB, which had come together to fight the 1967 election as the Independence Party, began to break up. The IFB left the government. Though the Prime Minister still had a majority, his position was weaker. He began to approach his main opponents, Gaëtan Duval and the PMSD, about the possibility of a coalition. Eventually, by December 1969, and after much dealing and compromise over government posts, the PMSD joined the Labour Party and the MCA to form a coalition government.

It must have seemed a strange development to some after the arguments between the two leaders in the 1967 election. Yet it had already happened once before and would happen again after 1976. There were good reasons in its favour. It strengthened the Prime Minister's position. Moreover, he had often appealed for national unity and called on Mauritians to work together in the country's interests. It would also lessen the chance of communal troubles between the racial groups represented by the three parties in the coalition. Finally, since independence was a reality, it was no longer an issue between the two parties.

Effect on Labour Party policy

It is important, however, to realise the less desirable consequences for the Labour Party of its coalition with the PMSD. The Labour Party was a party of the left with socialist ideals. Sir Seewoosagur advocated a more just distribution of the national wealth and was dedicated to the creation of a welfare state. Before independence many members of the party believed that the best way to achieve their objectives was through the nationalisation of the country's key industry, the sugar industry. Labour's new link with the PMSD made it impossible to implement such a programme. The PMSD's main support came from the country's business interests, including the sugar magnates, and the price of the new political alliance included the abandonment of nationalisation of the sugar industry. This did not necessarily mean that the Labour Party had abandoned its basic aim to redistribute more fairly the national income, but it did mean that the aim had to be achieved within the existing framework of a capitalist or, at best, a mixed economy. Some of the Labour Party's MPs and their supporters were unhappy about this compromise.

The big question, however, was how long would the coalition last. Doubts about the deal were not confined to members of the Labour Party. It led to an almost immediate split in the PMSD. Nearly half the party was opposed to joining the coalition and broke away to form the Union Democratique Mauricienne (UDM). Even some of Duval's colleagues who approved of the coalition were dissatisfied with the share of government posts offered to the party. Duval himself resigned for a time but returned to the Cabinet later as Foreign Minister.

The emergence of the MMM

However, the coalition survived uneasily until December 1973 and was useful to the Prime Minister during a period when a serious new threat to his political domination first emerged. This came in the shape of a new left-wing party, the Mouvement Militant Mauricien (MMM). Its founder was a young man, Paul Bérenger. He was the son of a well-to-do Franco-Mauritian family who had studied philosophy and journalism in Britain and France. He returned to Mauritius in 1968 imbued with revolutionary fervour after undergoing a dramatic political baptism at the barricades with the students and workers of Paris.

It was a time of ferment, especially amongst the young, in many countries, a time when demand for radical change was widespread. As a new political party in Mauritius, the emergence of the MMM came at a time when the coalition between Labour and the PMSD had left a vacuum of opposition. The MMM quickly filled that vacuum but in a very different form to the opposition previously supplied by the PMSD. The MMM was a party of the extreme left with a Marxist-Leninist ideology and a formidable party machine which, for the time being at least, operated outside Parliament. It was controlled by the Secretary-General and developed a powerful trade union wing. From the beginning the party had an appeal to the youth of the country and to the workers, mainly Creoles, in the docks. Slowly it broadened its base, spreading its appeal to the young elements in the 'general population' and to the Indian workers on the sugar estates. Its full strength, however, and its potential threat to the established pattern of political parties was not fully realised until it gained an overwhelming victory over a Labour opponent in the by-election at Triolet in September 1970. The effect of this was all the more striking because it was the Prime Minister's constituency, previously a stronghold of the Labour Party. The victorious candidate was a young Indo-Mauritian, Dev Virahsawmy, who symbolised for many the aspirations of young people for fundamental changes in society and who advocated the adoption of Creole as the national language of Mauritius.

The government's reaction was to defend its position by passing two amendments to the constitution. In future, vacancies in the Assembly would be filled automatically by a replacement from the party of the member who had vacated the seat. The date for the next general election, due in 1972, was postponed for four years.

Bérenger and the MMM turned their main energies towards winning influence and support in the trade unions. Again this threatened a traditional stronghold of the Labour Party. In June 1971 the party repeated its Triolet success in a municipal by-election and in September of the same year it won seats in sixteen out of twenty-seven villages where it put forward candidates.

A wave of strikes had broken out earlier in the year and were generally acknowledged to have been stirred up by MMM party members. Transport and other industries were seriously disrupted. Most serious of all was the dock strike. It began in early September and lasted for forty days. The MMM's main hope was that the government would be forced to call a general election. In fact the government passed the Public Order Act which allowed for the banning of political meetings and strengthened the powers of the police. After the dock strike, a state of emergency was proclaimed in December 1971. This was extended in the following year and the leaders of the MMM were held in detention. Strict control was

Sir Seewoosagur Ramgoolam addresses the opening of the OAU Summit in Mauritius, 1976

maintained over the activities of the party. The continued detention of its leaders helped the MMM to consolidate its support amongst radical groups in all communities. Eventually differences arose within the Cabinet over the extension of the state of emergency and the continued detention of the leaders of the MMM.

The government is strengthened 1974-1976

In 1973, however, the MMM itself was weakened by internal disagreements. The government felt more secure. Differences between Ramgoolam and Duval over issues of foreign policy, relating in particular to South Africa, had been played down by the Prime Minister as long as the danger from the MMM continued. By the end of 1973, however, the need for PMSD support was not so great. The Prime Minister himself took control of foreign affairs early in 1974. The government had the support of several ex-members of the PMSD and of the IFB who changed their allegiance to the Labour Party at this time. Economic and social reform remained the government's chief concern, but there were clear signs that the economic boom which had helped the government for several years was giving way to a recession.

As the time of the election approached, Mauritius became the stage for a series of special meetings which the government, no doubt, hoped would increase its prestige. In June 1976 the summit meeting of the Organisation of African Unity was held in Mauritius and Ramgoolam became the chairman of the organisation. Mrs Gandhi, the Indian Prime Minister, paid an official visit during which she opened the Mahatma Gandhi Institute, a symbol of the close cultural links between Mauritius and the subcontinent. In August the Institute housed the second Hindi Convention. At the meeting of heads of non-aligned states held in Colombo, Ramgoolam kept himself in the limelight of international affairs and received wide support over the issue of the American military base on Diego Garcia (see Chapter 18). Finally, in September, Mauritius once again became the venue for an international gathering: the meeting of the Commonwealth Parliamentary Association. Britain was strongly criticised for her handling of the Diego Garcia issue. A month later, on 21 October 1976, the Mauritius House of Assembly was dissolved. Early in November, the Prime Minister announced that the general election would be held on 20 December 1976.

The election of 1976

Although the Prime Minister's standing as a statesman of international reputation was very high, it was issues of domestic politics which mattered most to the voters. One of the government's recent decisions about this time was of major importance. Just a year before the election, the vote was given to eighteen-year-olds. It was a dangerous gamble as, in the upshot, it was the MMM, which had identified itself with youth, that profited the most from this revolutionary change, but for the Prime Minister it was an imaginative act of bold statesmanship and he has never regretted it.

Sir Seewoosagur made it clear at the time of the dissolution of the old assembly that he would fight the election on his record and achievements whilst in office. No outgoing prime minister can do otherwise. The MMM, whilst recognising that there had been achievements, insisted that they had not gone far enough: power and wealth in Mauritius were still monopolised by too few people. It promised radical reforms to transform society by redistributing wealth and placing the great sugar estates, insurance companies and docks under state control. The MMM did not entirely ignore foreign affairs. They seized on the two issues which were matters of some public concern and promised to break all links with South Africa and reclaim Diego Garcia.

Behind the scenes there were attempts by representatives of the Labour Party and the MMM to find common ground and make an electoral pact. The attempts failed, however, and, from then on, the differences between them were emphasised. The Prime Minister and his chief supporters tried to sell the Labour Party as a moderate socialist party and to denounce the MMM as communists and the PMSD as reactionary capitalists. The MMM branded the Labour Party as a bourgeois party in league with the sugar magnates.

No fewer than thirty-one parties put forward candidates, but only half a dozen were serious contenders. When the results were announced, only four parties had succeeded in gaining seats; the Labour Party and the MCA, who fought together as the Independence Party, the PMSD and the MMM.

For the MMM the election was almost a triumph: for the others it was almost a disaster and certainly a shock and a disappointment. The results were:

	Seats in main election	Percentage of vote	Seats reserved for 'best losers'	Total seats
Independence Party (Labour + MCA)	25	37.2	3	28
PMSD	7	16.5	1	8
MMM	30	40.1	4	34

The MMM was comfortably the largest single party. Its achievement was all the more remarkable in that it had not even existed at the time of the previous election. Its only weakness was that it had just failed, by two seats, to win an absolute majority over all other

Aucun parti n'a tenu la majorité absolue

● Malgré la conspiration des autres partis qui ont disparu de la scène politique, le Parti Travailliste a préservé son entité

● Le MMM a eu un bon score mais n'a pas atteint l'objectif visé

● Le gouvernement et le PMSD ont la majorité dans la nouvelle législature

Headlines after the election of December 1976

parties, a position which would have given it an undisputed right to form a government. It had equally failed, by a rather more decisive margin, to poll a majority of the votes. It had obtained 40 per cent of the votes cast.

There was also the shock of rejection by the electorate of so many of the ex-ministers. No fewer than ten Labour ministers lost their seats, though a few came back as 'best losers'. Gaëtan Duval also lost his seat, but his party was in the position of holding the balance between the two largest parties. Neither could govern without PMSD support. It was unthinkable that the MMM and the PMSD should join forces to form a government. Predictably, therefore, the outcome was likely to be a revival of the old coalition between the Independence Party and the PMSD.

Labour, PMSD coalition revived 1976

Bérenger, as leader of the largest single party, claimed the right to form a government. However, he had no such constitutional right. In a situation in which no party had an absolute majority, the retiring prime minister held the initiative and quickly let it be known that he was negotiating with Duval to form a coalition government. He succeeded more easily than he had in 1969. The need to keep the common foe out of power was greater in 1976 than it had been in 1969. Because Ramgoolam's need of PMSD support was also greater, he had to pay a higher price in terms of sharing office with his allies.

Bérenger and the MMM walked out of the first session of the new assembly in protest at what they regarded as unconstitutional manoeuvring. It may have been manoeuvring, but it was not unconstitutional. Bérenger was learning from a master of the art that 'Politics is the art of the possible'. In the long run, it has proved to have been to his advantage and that of the MMM. His party was a young party of men with little experience. They were given a chance to learn the art of politics and the ways of parliamentary procedure without the additional burden of office and the responsibility of governing.

Reasons for MMM's success

It has been suggested that the MMM's success was a victory for the unity of Mauritians of all races against communalism. Certainly the MMM received support from the workers of different communities and the support of idealists, especially young ones, from different races. There was evidence that some votes had been cast on class rather than communal lines, but this was not proof that communalism was dead and that it had ceased to operate in the 1976 election. The MMM owed some of its success to its recognition of the continuing strength of communalism. It skilfully put forward candidates whose race was likely to have maximum appeal in a particular constituency.

The MMM also had as President, Aneerood Jugnauth, which enabled it to acquire a wider support, particularly among the Hindus. Jugnauth was first elected under the IFB banner in 1963 and became a Minister in the pre-independence coalition government. He then gave up politics for some time and became a magistrate.

In the early 70's he returned to politics and joined the MMM. He was genuinely convinced that he had found a political base from which to lead a more effective fight for the improvement of the lot of the common man. That he was going to be Prime Minister in an MMM Government contributed significantly to the broadening of the MMM base and to the successes of the party in the 1976 and 1982 General Elections.

	Total	IP	PMSD	MMM
Hindus	39	22	–	17
Creoles	19	4	6	9
Muslims	9	2	–	7
Chinese	1	–	–	1
Franco-Mauritians	2	–	2	–

Membership of the Assembly broken down into racial terms

The table shows that the MMM had successful candidates from every racial group except the Franco-Mauritians. The MMM had much working class support but it is not true that class had replaced communalism as the basis of politics.

What was the explanation of the results of the 1976 election in which the older parties did so badly and the new, untried MMM came so near to complete victory? It was an advantage to the MMM that it was a new and untried party. The Labour Party had held power for too long; ever since independence and for ten years before that. They had achieved much; but for many of their followers it was not enough. Those who were disappointed, who felt that too little had changed, were ready to give a new party a chance to show what they could do. They wanted to see new men in the House of Assembly. What happened in Mauritius in 1976 had happened before in the democratic world. The wonder was, not that the Labour Party had lost seats, but that it still retained the means of holding power.

There was some evidence that the MMM's success in the parliamentary election was not just a freak result on a particular occasion. Urban council elections were held in April 1977 and, in these, the MMM's performance was even more successful than in the general election. Their candidates won seats even in the wealthier suburbs. They gained control of Port Louis, Beau Bassin-Rose Hill and of Vacoas-Phoenix. Only in Quatre Bornes and Curepipe were the MMM defeated by the PMSD and the Independence Party campaigning jointly as a single party.

The emergence of the PSM

The world economy had started to go through a depression and along with this the price of oil rose and that of sugar fell. The Mauritian rupee was devalued twice but the social benefits of the Welfare State were not curtailed. The burden became almost unbearable.

At the same time, after the 1976 General Elections, there was a strong current in the country in favour of a renewal of the Labour Party through a thorough review of its organisation and structure. Harish Boodhoo, a young newly elected member, symbolized, in the minds of many people, the great desire for change in an effort to re-vitalize the Party and to re-establish its credentials with the people. The 'old guard' however resisted any proposal for change.

In the absence of progress along these lines Harish Boodhoo decided to set up the *Parti Socialiste Mauricien* (PSM). The PSM gained momentum and allied with the MMM to fight the Labour Party and the PMSD in the June 1982 General Elections.

The results of the June 1982 elections in fact showed a total swing to the MMM/PSM alliance which won all the seats in Mauritius (42 MMM and 18 PSM). The two seats in Rodrigues were captured by the *Organisation du Peuple Rodriguais* (OPR). The Labour Party and the PMSD suffered their worst set back, with neither of these parties returning any elected candidate. However the 'corrective' element in the constitution gave these two parties a total of four 'best losers' to represent the least represented communities in the Legislative Assembly. The second batch of four best losers could not be 'elected', the machinery breaking down as all the MMM/PSM candidates had been elected. Aneerood Jugnauth, President of the MMM became Prime Minister, Harish Boodhoo, leader of the PSM, Deputy-Prime Minister and Paul Bérenger, Secretary-General of the MMM, Minister of Finance.

The MMM/PSM Government

The new government was immediately faced with towering economic and social problems. There was no likelihood of an early solution to the problem of unemployment. The prescriptions of the International Monetary Fund (I.M.F.) and the World Bank to redress the economy were unpalatable, but the Government had to accept most of the conditions laid down by these two institutions before being granted much-needed loans.

The break-up of the alliance

After a few months of power-sharing, cracks began to appear in the MMM/PSM alliance and these widened. The alliance finally broke up in March 1983, with the MMM suffering a severe split in the process.

Several reasons have been advanced for the break-up. There was no opposition worth the name after the June election, so opposition came from within. Some of the new government's measures were unpopular and some of its members were reluctant to defend and stand by them. Finally there was a constitutional crisis. The Prime Minister wished to abide by the constitution of the country whilst Bérenger and the MMM politbureau pressed him to abide by the constitution of the party. It was in fact this crisis that precipitated the split in the government and within the MMM.

Internationally the sympathies of the government for left wing regimes did not encourage investment from capitalist countries. The result was that the economic and social situation did not improve.

The August 1983 General Elections

When the alliance broke up and the MMM split in March 1983, Jugnauth constituted another government and carried on until July when he announced that a General Election would be held on 21 August 1983.

In the meantime Jugnauth and Boodhoo launched a new party, the *Movement Socialiste Militant* (MSM), with the backing of the PSM and that section of the MMM which had remained loyal to Jugnauth.

The MSM allied with the Labour Party and had a working arrangement with the PMSD to fight the MMM.

The results of the elections gave a comfortable majority to Jugnauth who formed a new MSM-LABOUR PARTY-PMSD-OPR Government. The results of the elections were as follows:

MSM/L.P.	—	37
P.M.S.D.	—	4
O.P.R.	—	2
MMM	—	19

The government, like the previous one, saw its essential task as reviving the economy and solving the problem of unemployment. Sir Aneerood Jugnauth stated his belief in democratic socialism and parliamentary democracy, pledging that the policies of the MSM would protect and strengthen democracy. The MSM's economic programme, he added, was to promote free enterprise, but within a mixed economy which would temper the workings of free market capitalism with government intervention to protect the poorer sections of the community.

From 1983 to the Elections of August 1987

Between 1983 and 1987, Mauritius made enormous economic strides forward. Figures published by an IMF Report in February 1987 showed that the Gross National Product had risen from 3% in 1980 to 6% in 1986, while inflation had decreased dramatically, from 33% to 4.3% during the same period. The new "zone franche" industries had transformed the economy and by the middle of 1987 there was nearly full employment and inflation had come right down to under 1%. It was a substantial achievement and put the government in a very strong position to face the electorate.

A General Election was fixed for 30 August 1987. The government presented essentially the same team as in 1983, the MSM-Labour-PMSD coalition based its appeal on its economic record as well as on the ideological claim that Jugnauth had saved the country from a "one-party" dictatorship. During these years, a serious drugs problem had also surfaced in the country and the government was able to claim that it had taken decisive action in dealing with the problem by implementing the essence of the Rault Commission's Report, especially its anti-corruption recommendations.

On the opposition side, it was generally assumed that the charismatic leader of the MMM, Paul Bérenger, would once again put himself forward as the opposition candidate for Prime Minister. However, in an attempt to come to terms with the realities of electoral politics in Mauritius, Bérenger and the MMM opted to bring in a Hindu, Dr Prem Nababsing, as their choice for the top job in politics.

The electoral campaign himself was very vigorous though it showed a welcome decrease in the personal bitterness that had marked the 1983 elections. In terms of the number of people attending party political rallies – the traditional barometer of Mauritian political support – both sides seemed neck and neck going into the final week of the campaign. According to Jugnauth's biographer, Kevin Shillington, it was the outgoing Prime Minister's final television broadcast, just a few hours before the polls opened, which may have proved decisive.[1] In this broadcast Jugnauth warned of dire consequences resulting from MMM's proposed constitutional changes: the establishment of a Republic with new powers being conferred on the future President – in all likelihood Bérenger himself – would, he implied, make the latter once again the most powerful person in the running of the country's affairs. This may well have had the desired effect on the Hindu electorate.

On a poll of 85%, voting returns confirmed pre-election predictions as to the closeness of the two political groupings with Jugnauth's alliance emerging only one and three-quarter percentage points ahead. However, under the first-past-the-post electoral system, he was able to emerge with 39 of the 62 contested seats. After the allocation of the best-loser seats, Jugnauth's MSM/Labour/PMSD Alliance held 46 seats in the Assembly to the MMM's 24, though the latter remained the largest single party. Bérenger himself lost in Quatre-Bornes, remaining Secretary-General of the MMM outside Parliament, with Nababsing taking over as Leader of the Opposition in the new Assembly.

Between 1983 and 1987 Jugnauth had considerably widened his range of support. The stability and material prosperity which had become the hallmark of his government was, by 1987, attracting the support of the Chinese community, businessmen from all ethnic groups, middle-class Creoles, as well as

1 *Kevin Shillington, Jugnauth: Prime Minister of Mauritius (Macmillan 1991), p. 169.*

the Civil Service. Jugnauth had moved some way towards his aim of creating a single national movement that would cut across the old communal divides and still give him a clear majority.

Political, Social and Economic developments since 1987

In early 1990, amidst rumours of an impending electoral pact between the MMM and Labour, Jugnauth took most political commentators by surprise when he successfully negotiated an alliance with the MMM. The terms of the agreement included, at the MMM's insistence, a constitutional change that would turn Mauritius into a Republic. Most of the Labour ministers were, at this point, dismissed or handed in their resignation. A minority, however, refused to follow the line of the party leader, Sir Satcam Boolell and stayed in govern-ment, forming at the same time a break-away Labour group, the MTD (Mouvement des Travaillistes Démocratiques). The General Election of 1991 saw a comfortable win for the MSM/MMM Alliance with Jugnauth remaining Prime Minister, and Bérenger joining the Cabinet as Minister of Foreign Affairs. Cassam Uteem, a former member of the MMM, became the first president of the new Republic.

Meanwhile, on the economic front, techno-logical innovations in the island's main industry, sugar, have pushed it into second place as the major wage and export earner. And the expansion of water provision and the increase in electricity generation has sustained the industrial development that remains the government's chief source of pride. Planning for future requirements in terms of electricity and water include the construction of additional reserves that will provide a regular and reliable water supply in every household throughout the year; the extension of the existing water network so as to cope with the increasing demand of industrial and domestic water; increased use of the island's natural energy resources; and an improved network that will ensure that every household has its own electricity supply.

Economic growth has led to an impressive rise in living standards. There have been substantial improvements in housing, in clothing, and in the ownership of consumer goods such as refrigerators, television sets, and cars. In 1989 there was a network of 74,000 telephones on the island – i.e. over one out of every three households. Infant mortality has declined from 65-70 per 1,000 births in the late 1960s to 21.6 per 1,000 in 1989. However, some pockets of poverty, especially in the south west of the island, do still remain. For instance, all the major social indicators for the Black River District suggest relative deprivation amongst sections of its population.

Economic growth has also led to fundamental social change. There is now much greater mobility in Mauritian society than 20 years ago. Parents entertain greater ambitions for the children and economic progress has increased the range of jobs and occupations on offer. New enterprises and businesses seem less concerned with ethnic origin in their hiring policies and much keener on academic and technical qualifi-cations. As a result, young people generally feel justified in entertaining higher aspirations than their parents did in the previous generation.

Arguably, Mauritius is becoming much more of a western-style competitive society than a 'traditional' third world society. The demographic structure of the country has now begun to resemble that of industrial societies. In the early 1960s many observers of Mauritian society expected a population explosion, as a result of the decline in the death rate brought about by the elimination of malaria in the 1950s. However, this did not happen: from an average of 40.7 per thousand in 1956-60 and 38.6 per thousand in 1961-65, the birth rate had fallen to 20 by 1989.

This decline in the birth rate is also related to an increase in the average age of marriage. Twenty years ago, it was common for women to be married before they reached the age of 20; in 1986, less than a quarter of women getting married were under 20 years old. Again, two decades ago, families with six children or more were common; nowadays families of two or three are more typical. The gradual ageing of the population which is a feature of industrial societies is also happening in Mauritius. In 1967, 43.5% of the population were under 15 years of age; by 1989 this proportion had fallen to 29.9%.

At the same time there has also been a fundamental change in the position of women. Twenty years ago, there was little employment available outside domestic service or work in the sugar-cane fields. To-day, the recently established manufacturing and service industries employ a great number of women. In the Export Processing Zone (the "zone franche" which contains the major export industries), 67% of all employees in 1990 were women. Girls are also staying longer at school: in 1989, girls comprised almost 50% of the school population.

In the field of education, the government abolished University fees in 1988, thus extending free education to the tertiary level following the introduction, by Sir Seewoosagur Ramgoolam's Government, of free secondary schooling in 1977. The education system has been able to deliver the manpower needs of Mauritian industrialisation while broadening the range of studies at all levels. The multilingual and multicultural nature of Mauritian society has been recognised in the emphasis given to the teaching of community languages. A wider range of subjects are now taught at secondary level, while the University has recently expanded its range of degree courses.

While Sir Seewoosagur Ramgoolam had been able to create political independence and national unity out of communal strife and had laid the groundwork for a potential industrial revolution, Sir Aneerood Jugnauth has shown the skill and vision to build upon that solid foundation and transform the Mauritian economy into one that is the envy of much of the modern world. Much of course remains to be done: but prospects for the future seem bright.

Suggestions for revision

You should know:

a) the results of the elections of 1967, 1976, 1982, 1983 and 1987 and the reasons for these results;
b) the different party combinations which enabled first Sir Seewoosagur Ramgoolam and then Sir Aneerood Jugnauth to form governments since 1968;
c) the story behind the emergence and rise of the MMM and the explanation of its performance in the 1976 election;
d) the reasons for the emergence of the MSM and its performance in the 1987 election.

Suggestions for further work

1 This chapter covers events and developments in the most recent period of the history of Mauritius, a period through which you have probably lived. This does not mean that the events are easier to understand. In some ways, the reverse is true. It does mean, however, that it is comparatively easy to look back through accounts and reports of these events in recent newspapers. Apart from telling parts of the story in much more detail than has been done in this book, newspaper accounts may differ, both from each other and from the short account here. If they do, what may be the reasons for the differences? What does this teach you about the work of the historian whose task is to tell the story as accurately as possible and, at the same time, to give some explanation of why things happened as they did? What is the difference between the task of a newspaper editor or a newspaper reporter and that of a historian writing about important events like the General Elections of 1982 and 1983 in Mauritius?

2 Make sure you know the meaning of the following words: socialist (page 110), capitalist (page 113) and bourgeois (page 113).

INDEX